Carole

remembering

&

forgetting

a memoir and other pieces of my life

by

miriam spiegel raskin

This is a compilation of pieces I wrote over many years in an effort to come to terms with the sadness in my experience of the world. I dedicate it to all the innocents I drew into my sadness with me and who eventually helped me to overcome it with their unending love and support.

Some parts have been previously published in *The Sagarin Review, Simcha Magazine, First Harvest: Jewish Writing in St. Louis 1991-1997, First Harvest: Jewish Writing in St. Louis 1998-2005, New Harvest, The St. Louis Jewish Light,* and other publications.

ISBN#1-4196-8952-5

Published by Booksurge.org

January 2008

CONTENTS

part 1: memoir:

Remembering & Forgetting

Remembering	10
A Joke	18
The Funeral	20
Being Jewish	24
Kristallnacht	37
Moving On	39
Getting Tough	44
A Good Girl	47
Adaptations	50
An Ordinary Day	53
In Lieu of Kaddish	58
Forgetting	63
Calm Nights	68
Getting Religion	72
Funtime	76
Like a Sickness	80
Objective Analysis	84
Suite 1000	88
Dreaming	92
Not Yet	97
Afterword	100

CONTENTS

part 2: poems

Resuffering	104
Psalm 1987	105
Letter from Home	107
Around the World in 80 Years	108
American Girl	109
Beads of Perfection	110
In the Beginning	111
Giving Life to the Dead	112
July Mourning	114
Mother's Day	116
Kadosh Kadosh	121
If I Should Die Before I Wake	122
Maker of Peace	123
A Good Thing	124
Early Morning	127
Choose Life	128
I Am What I Am	130

part 3: essays

All Things Considered	132
Too Good To Be True	145
Meeting the Other, Finding It's Me	160
The Appeal of Unconsciousness	164
Eschstrasse 19	169
Coda	175

memoir

remembering

and forgetting

[written 1988-1990]

remembering and forgetting

REMEMBERING

I don't remember. I say it only because it is true, not to boast or to complain. I simply don't remember what happened five minutes ago, or, for that matter, five decades ago, and I have as much trouble retaining good memories as bad ones. Every experience vanishes: the beautiful and the ugly, the painful and the joyful, the commonplace and the exceptional. It is not of my choosing, this personal deficit no one but I takes seriously. People closest to me, who should know better, often suggest that I forget on purpose and that I could remember if I just paid attention, if I just chose to remember. They are wrong: I do choose to remember.

With unflagging effort, I stir and stir the teeming cauldron of my life's brew, searching among the bubbling flotsam for bits and pieces of my personal identity. From that dark reservoir in which childhood treasures and torments lie hidden, side by side, I hope to draw clues to important events, important people, in my life. I want to remember, more than any thing, any one else, Oma, my maternal grandmother. Wonderful as I am told she was, I would cherish fond memories of her, if I had any. I have none..Although I am the youngest survivor of all those she

remembering and forgetting

ever loved, I must depend on the memories of my elders.

The eyes of her daughters still glisten when they speak of her. They remember. To listen to them, she was at once an angel, goodness incarnate, compassion made womanly flesh. More: she was a loving wife to a man she did not love, a conscientious homemaker and a devoted mother all the while that her instincts and her attributes were more those of an artist, a seductress, an empress, a saint.

Over and over, I try to summon up my own memories of her. In the penultimate solitude of sleepless nights, I strain to recapture the configuration of her face as she looked into mine, not necessarily the last time, when she must have known that we were unlikely to see one another again, but any time, any one instant of the many days of companionship that we shared, especially during the long weeks following the trauma of Kristallnacht when we took refuge in her Hamburg apartment, counting neither on God nor man but only on the statistical probability that the Nazis would fill their quotas for rounding up Jewish males before they searched the dark back room in which my father was sequestered. She and I certainly talked to each other during those harrowing days, each searching for answers we would not find. I must have known her face intimately then but, try as I will, I cannot pull the tiniest fragment of her living image up to the dark screen of my mind.

So it is that I remember my grandmother only as she appears in two photographs that stand on a small shelf in my mother's house. In one picture I see an old woman in dark, old-woman clothes, her lined face encircled by coarse gray hair, unstylish but pleasant looking. Her figure is ungainly beside the small child whose hand she holds. She stands as a mass of solid support for the child balancing herself with care on a narrow stone ledge bordering a flowerbed. That little girl was some earlier discrete form of me, I am told, although that is another perception of reality

remembering and forgetting

that I cannot confirm by personal recollection.

I stare at the picture hoping to recall the experience it captures. Despite the rationally acceptable evidence of my physical presence in the scene, I cannot remember the frozen instant or the days that surrounded it. I was spending a summer holiday alone with my grandparents during some good days I am told preceded the bad times. That day may well have been a perfect, blissful, halcyon day of untarnished innocence. I don't really remember.

In defiance of my nature, I do have a homely memory of my grandfather, a stern-visaged man with wire-rimmed spectacles who looked every inch the proud bank officer he wanted me to believe he was. ("He was a clerk," my mother, his daughter, says. "He was something like a teller, certainly not an official of any kind." She is more than a little ashamed of this truth she must share with me.)

I remember how he bounced me on his knee when I was very small and how he compared the nether parts of my anatomy to his favorite *Franzbrötchen*, a breakfast roll named to honor the Kaiser on whose behalf he had rushed to the battlefield to fight and be wounded in an era when Jews could still be Germans. .Although the knee-bouncing incident is no impressive memory, I cling to it. .It is all I have and, what is more, I like remembering the unloved husband as a fond grandfather. Especially, I like remembering.

The second photograph of my grandmother is a formal portrait by a second-rate photographer whose livelihood had rested on passport photos until the Nazis put an end to passports. She looks straight out of this picture, with fear and determination, at the future which holds no promise for her. We were safe by then, having reached the golden shores by a combination of luck and circumstance that lifetimes of earthly virtue could not merit. I wonder now what went through our minds when that picture, the

remembering and forgetting

last, arrived in the fragile, censored airmail envelope unmarked by the despair of those who sent it on its way. Did I know then that I would never see her again? that the photos would stop coming, and then the letters, and then, nothing, nothing at all?

How was I to know? I was a child, protected from the discussion of such morbid reflections as the times called for. I heard no prophecies of doom from my mother, herself barely beyond childhood when she left her beloved, adored mother to cross the seas with child and husband to start life anew on safer ground. If she suspected her adieu to be a final one, she never let on, never.

She did not say a word. When the letters stopped arriving, our life went on as usual. There was no Western Union message to start the wailing, to justify the recitation of the Kaddish. .When the day came that we knew for a fact that my grandparents were no longer alive, that their earthly remains had long before been incorporated into Russian soil, our loss seemed unworthy of much notice. The dimensions of the known catastrophe were by then too large to warrant attention, even our own, to our small suffering. The kind of self-centeredness that would have let us weep for two souls out of six million was not part of the family character. We did not weep and thereby gave up weeping.

Perhaps, if we had wept, if we had been able to weep, I could have stopped looking for my grandmother long ago. Instead, though I am now older than she was when I last saw her, the child in me still pauses to stare at old women in dark, old-woman clothes and awaits the impossible miracle of recognition and reunion. But she is dead and, even in the natural course of events, should be dead by now. Her being dead is not really the problem. People die and those that remain go on living. That is the way it is and must be.

This is the problem. I have heard many impressive stories about my grandmother. About the time that she

≈13≈

traveled alone to the battleground to look for my grandfather who had been reported missing in action and managed to find him among heaps of wounded soldiers. About the people in trouble that she helped with money and favors when she barely had enough for herself. About the men that she loved and did not marry and about the social and cultural and personal aspirations that were thwarted but never abandoned. I have heard and reheard such wonderful stories about her, in English and in German, over the years but, fascinating as they are, I listen to them with half an ear; I cannot relate to them.

The stories about my grandmother's life serve only to remind me of her death. The only story that compels my attention is the one that I will never hear, the one about her death-in-life, the one that describes the indescribable, unknown and unknowable terrors that my grandmother, who should have been a siren or a saint but got stuck instead in mundane living and grotesque death, was forced to endure. Multiplying that finite unknown by a factor of six million produces the absolute mystery of human existence in our time. It is the mystery that transcends all stories ever told, all questions ever asked, all memories ever remembered or forgotten. In truth, it stands in the way of story telling, of remembering and, most of all, of living.

Against the shadow of that dark mystery, it is hard for me to fret about the fact that I do not remember, whether for psychological reasons or others, more limiting and even less reversible. Against that mystery, it matters little what I remember or do not remember, what I think or do not think, or, in the final analysis, what I do or do not do.

Nothing matters, nothing that is within my power to do has the capacity to matter. Still, one must live and so I do. And to the best of my ability, I live AS IF.

<u>*remembering and forgetting*</u>

AS IF I shared my mother's happier view of life.
>AS IF I could make a difference in the world.
>AS IF my life mattered.
>AS IF it was worth saving.

≈≈≈

remembering and forgetting

A JOKE

My parents had a joke and I was it. I was born, they said, nine months and ten days after they were married, and they had been "careful". I was duly amused and almost flattered by the occasional utterance of this information because it was unusual for my parents to share details of their personal lives with me. They must have thought themselves daring and witty and almost *avant garde* to make references to contraception and even to failed contraception to their young daughter. It made me feel sophisticated, wise beyond my years, to think they took me to understand what being careful meant. I didn't know, of course. I only knew that whatever caution they had exercised had failed and they had ended up with me. A burden. They never said that but I knew.

"Oh, darling," my aunt says to me with the heavy German accent that she will never lose, "I can still see my mother -- your grandmother -- the day the letter came from my sister. It was summer, a few months after their wedding and your parents were living in that tiny apartment in Hagen where I later came to visit you, do you remember? and your father was barely making enough money to keep a family of birds alive, and this letter comes -- I can see my

remembering and forgetting

mother's face as she opens it -- 'Oh, no,' she cries, 'I don't believe this, if I had known, if I had had the slightest idea they would be so foolish, I would never have permitted them to marry. Listen to this,' she says, 'listen,' and she reads to me what your mother wrote, in her prissy style, '"Dear mother and father, You might as well start imagining yourselves as grandparents in December."'"

My aunt purses up her mouth and lifts her head to achieve a more patrician demeanor as she quotes the letter. "That's the way my sister told her mother she was pregnant. What a shock it was to her. 'Do you believe it,' my mother wailed, 'in these times, with these ruffians trying to take over the country, that these babies should think of having a child?' Oh, I can tell you, she was stunned. She was more than stunned, she was devastated by the news. And she meant it," she says, with emphasis. "She would not have let your parents get married, if she had known."

My aunt goes on like this but my mother holds her tongue. She smiles wryly as her sister does her Tom Smothers act, still trying to prove how close she and her mother were, more than half a century ago.

"What could she have done," my mother asks at last, "We were not children. We wanted to be married."

It was 1930 when they got married, were careful, and then, before they had a chance to plan for one, had a child to take care of. My heart reaches out to those young people, my parents, struggling to make a home for a child they were not prepared to have in the midst of the political and economic turmoil of the times. I imagine how difficult it was for them, trying to be grownup and self-sufficient, away from their own nests for the first time, she barely twenty and he twenty-five, and burdened with this baby, me, carrying the weight of the universe in her eyes.

As if it was not bad enough for them to have to worry,

remembering and forgetting

behind closed doors, how they could possibly stretch my father's meager profits from a small textile establishment to unexpected lengths or what would happen to the Jews if the Nazis came to power, they suddenly (so it must have seemed to them) had to contend with this child that did not laugh, this serious, serious child that was always trailing after them, waiting for something, wanting something she never named.

"*Was tust Du nun?*", I used to ask at very short intervals. What are you going to do now? And then? and after that?

They would sit me down to play and surround me with toys and books, hoping to go about their own business. Moments later, I would be up again, standing at their sides again, asking that question again. What are you going to do now? and then? and then? In their innocence they took my questioning at face value, perceiving me to be insatiably curious about what was going on around me, and they kept sitting me down again to amuse myself again, alone again, by myself again. (It only happened once, my mother says now, and not at all the way I've described it. What happened, she says, is that one day a neighbor we were visiting promised to give me a cookie but instead kept on talking and talking and I, after waiting patiently a long while, asked timidly, softly, "What are you going to do now? and after that, what?" until the woman remembered her promise, and gave me the cookie. But she is wrong, my mother is, in remembering it this way; she has forgotten how they teased me for asking that question all the time, how inquisitive I seemed to them, and how needy I was, not for a cookie, but for involvement in their activities, in their lives.)

I do not mean to criticize my parents, even indirectly. They were understandably confused by my seriousness and disappointed at my lack of enthusiasm for play. That I did

≈18≈

remembering and forgetting

not have a natural affinity to dolls was something of a shock to my mother, who at 80 is still more playful than I, who still has in her eyes the most remarkable sparkle that I altogether covet. She remembers herself as a happy child, playing for endless hours with dolls she loved so much and so long that a favorite had quite naturally accompanied her into marriage to grace her marital bed. And she remembers, always she remembers, how disappointed she was to discover, as a young mother unable to imagine that her own child would reject her childhood pleasures, that I was made of sterner stuff.

Which is what happened one year when she bought, with a sense of considerable abandonment of the notions of thrift to which she generally adhered, an extravagant doll carriage for me as a Chanukah gift. Excited about her purchase and eager to share it with me, she agonized through the weeks that it remained stored in the back of a stockroom of my father's store. She let herself in now and then to take another quiet look, to admire its elegant beauty once more while she endured the wait for the night when she could present it to me, and then, when Chanukah finally came, and on this our recollections agree, when the moment of presentation actually arrived and she held her breath in anticipation of my shrieks of joy, I took one look at the elegant carriage, pointed at the brown paper wrapping still covering the rubber wheels and asked, "Why is there paper on the wheels?"

Yes, I think I actually remember that moment and not just her oft-repeated recounting of the event. I can see myself, five, six years old and standing in the doorway of a stockroom looking beyond to the next room into which my mother had rushed, urging me on, and seeing in one instant the still partially wrapped carriage and the look of disappointment on her face when I spoke, her mouth falling open in shock at my lack of affect. The look is easy to recognize in retrospect; I have seen it so often since, and on so many faces.

    What did it mean, this irreversible moment, this superrational response to a highly charged transaction? I had merely responded in the fashion natural to me, checking out the salient facts to avoid any unhappy future revelations. Before I could risk expressing pleasure at the gift, I needed answers to the questions buzzing in my head: Was this a good carriage? why did it have paper on the wheels? was it meant for me? was it worth the money it cost?

    Emotionally, I took no risks. It was better to be safe than sorry, and perhaps better even to be safe than happy. Being safe was all that mattered. Forget the presents, the parties, the celebrations, make the world safe for me, I would have cried, had I not been too sensible to ask my parents to give what it was not in their power to give.

≈≈≈

remembering and forgetting

THE FUNERAL

When my darling great-grandfather died in 1936, I was five years old and already impressed for life. He was a tiny man, perhaps five foot two or three, and he lived, with a wife I remember not at all, on the third floor of the apartment building in Hamburg that also housed their daughter, my Oma Josephi.

Of course, I don't really remember him. That goes without saying. But we liked each other, that I know. And a few ancient photographs with scalloped edges testify to our occasional outings to the city's lush botanical gardens during our family visits to Hamburg. The old photos show him dressed in a dark three piece suit for his appointment with me, his face crinkling to what must have been my constant delight, as we walked through the park, inhaling the fragrant aromas of untold numbers of uncommon flora. I see him holding my hand as I balanced on the cast iron rails that surrounded the geometrically precise plantings. I imagine him listening gravely to my questions about the universe, never tiring of my childish prattle. I loved him, I suppose, although I did not know much about love.

He dressed formally as a matter of course and, as a matter of principle, wore a skullcap in the house. Rare as it was in our proudly assimilated family, he wore it as an

remembering and forgetting

emblem of his individuality, of his faith, and of his hopes for his family. Usually, it was plain and black but on Friday nights, when the dining table was adorned with the finest silver and the most elegant linens, a beautifully embroidered white *Kaeppelchen* covered his head when he took his place at the head of the table. I can still feel the hush settling around the table when he lifted the kiddush cup and held it high, and still marvel how from his undersized body there could emanate such a grandeur of spirit that the entire familial assemblage was drawn, almost against its will, into passionate Shabbat blessings and lusty renditions of *Ose Shalom Bim Ramov*, so that for those inspired moments this slight, unimposing little man mysteriously became a coalescing force, a model of noble character and a tower of strength. My mother fills me in on the facts.

"Do you know what he did for a living, this hero of yours?" asks my mother. "He did this and that. The most important thing he ever did in his life was nothing more impressive than delivering bread door to door for a local bakery. He was never very lucky in life."

No? But he was lucky in death. He was so lucky as to die in bed of an ordinary illness at a reason-able age, never knowing, never guessing, how unfounded his faith was to prove, lucky enough to die before the gates of hell opened to bring grisly unimaginable deaths to his children. Thank God for that, my mother would say, but I, less generous, more unforgiving, do not bring those words to my lips. He was lucky, that was all. As were we, I suppose, in not knowing when he died, and we grieved, that his interment in the Jewish graveyard of Hamburg with the customary blessings would be the last such family burial for decades to come.

I was not there to witness the somber occasion. My parents deferred to the prevailing views on child

remembering and forgetting

development and judged me to be too young to attend the funeral. Let's protect the child from the sadness, they thought, and left me in the care of a neighbor. Let's protect the child from the grief, they thought, and kept their own locked inside themselves. So it was that, doubly protected and doubly bereft, I missed what turned out to be the last family funeral for forty five years, the Nazis having assumed responsibility for dispensing with the remains of all the family members who died in the intervening years as a matter of neatness and public health when they did the killings that caused the deaths.

What they told me then I don't know. What I felt then I do not know but I suspect it was grief, real grief of the sort our family deemed somehow *declassé*, for even now, when I am myself an old woman, the strains of *Ose Shalom Bim Ramov* sometimes overwhelm me with such sweet sorrow that tears flow from my eyes in the most harmonious of circumstances and I imagine I can see, through the embarrassing inexplicable tears, my great-grandfather's delicate-as-Dresden-china face at the head of that long ago Shabbat table leading us all in song. And then I am grateful for the memory, thankful to be reminded that once, long ago, before death on a cosmic scale intruded into our family history, it included this exceptional specimen, this ordinary man who was my great-grandfather.

≈≈≈

remembering and forgetting

BEING JEWISH

It was the first night of Chanukah and I was a few days short of six when my father used his influence within the Synagogue of Bünde to have me lead the congregation in blessing the candles. He held my hand as I clambered onto the wooden crate placed for my sake behind the podium of the synagogue, helped me light a candle with a long wooden match and then retreated to a front row seat. I held my breath for a moment and then, standing shakily on the tips of my toes to look out over the podium, I chanted the traditional Hebrew blessings while raising the flaming candle to pass its fire to the first Chanukah candle.

Gingerly, I replaced the *shammos* (the Hebrew word means "servant") into its perch on the silver menorah. Holding a scrap of paper on which my father had typed the words, I began reciting this romantic, sad little poem dedicated to the shammos candle:

> With its flame this little candle
> set its fellows all aglow
> and for that, the little candle's
> dubbed a servant, we all know.

remembering and forgetting

> Far apart it is forced to stand --
> segregated from its brothers --
> looking darkness in the face
> while it offers light to others.
>
> The same is true of my poor people
> as it is for this small light n whose
> shimmering, wavering flames
> the history of Israel waxes bright.
>
> We Jews have lit the human spirit
> with the purest flame of God,
> and for that, our little people's
> thought less than human,
> and more than odd.

What my father was thinking when he selected these verses for me to recite I wish I knew. I never thought to ask and now it is too late. There is no clue of authorship in the faded lines that stare at me from the same fragile scrap of paper I held so many years ago although it occurs to me now that perhaps it was composed by the great Heinrich Heine, the German Jewish poet he so much admired even though he took Jewishness to be a plague shlepped back from the banks of the Nile.

My father had not reached that dour philosophical position but his mood must have been perfectly reflected in the bittersweet tone of my Chanukah recitation. Being Jewish in the Germany of 1936 gave even unthoughtful people a lot to think about, and my father was by nature reflective, contemplative almost to excess, or so my mother sometimes thought as she went about the business of doing, pursuant to their unspoken agreement which divided their religious responsibilities into conventional public/private domains. Public Jewishness was his concern.

The tiny Jewish community of Bünde in Westphalia -- we three comprised one of its thirty-odd families -- could boast of a substantial synagogue as the result of the largesse of Jewish residents of a prior generation, among them the legendary Julius Rosenwald, then and there in the cigar manufacturing business and later a founder of the Sears Roebuck dynasty in America. My father, who had no largesse to distribute and who was not a religious man even before the death of God became a prime topic for philosophical speculation, was nonetheless sufficiently attached to the tradition of his forefathers to carry out the responsibilities of the presidency of the synagogue. He was a Jew and proudly so, even if my mother's prescriptions for living Jewishly sometimes struck him as a trifle excessive for the intellectually enlightened age in which we lived.

Not that my mother had come from an orthodox household; on the contrary, her parents had themselves rebelled against the orthodoxy of an earlier time by unbinding themselves from what seemed to be excessive religious strictures without in any way weakening their sense of themselves as observant Jews. Relying more on instinct than any profound intellectual processing, they developed a new religious tradition of their own, just as binding as the old one, so that it was a foregone conclusion that when the time came for her to set up her own household, my mother would follow her mother's practices and customs for keeping the Jewish holy days holy. Which is what she did.

Exactly like her mother before her, she honored the Sabbath with candles and festive dinners and with abstention from the performance of major domestic chores. Exactly like her mother, she felt good about modernizing orthodox commandments and restrictions so that we could honor the Sabbath without, let's be frank, being ridiculous

remembering and forgetting

about it. Unlike the orthodox Eastern European Jews whose very presence embarrassed us whenever we saw them walking the streets in their unfashionable black garments, exhibiting their archaic rituals and mannerisms, we were free to turn lights on and off on the Sabbath, to cook and ride in elevators and cars and do all the ordinary small chores that daily life required. But turning on a washing machine, running a vacuum cleaner on the Sabbath, that was out of the question, is out of the question, in my mother's religion.

The dietary laws were likewise reduced to the level of suggestions. Uninspired to keep a kosher kitchen, my mother honored what she took to be the essence of *Kashrut*. She saw to it that we ate no pork or shellfish at any time through the year and that we abstained from eating leavened bread and cake during the week of Passover without ever considering for a moment that there was any dereliction of duty connected to not keeping separate sets of dishes for milk and meat foods. It was like keeping kosher under a new and improved redefinition, better suited to the times. My father was content to go along with my mother's choices in these matters, believing both that he had no authority to intervene in domestic matters and that the restrictions my mother chose to exemplify our Jewishness were more than adequate for the purpose of reminding us that we were Jews and obligated to live our lives in the prophetic tradition.

So it came down to this: although our family scrupulously obeyed very few commandments beyond the original Ten, we took seriously the moral imperatives we believed to be the heart of Judaism. All in all, it was a practical religion for us, one which allowed us to aim for the good life, in the original meaning of those words, without setting us too far apart from our neighbors, none of whom were Jewish. One was in fact a brown-shirted storm trooper whose uniform early caught my attention and whose daughter I still remember because, like no one else I ever knew, she stood always with one hand clinging to the lower edge of her underpants, pulling up her skirt and throwing her entire appearance into constant and permanent disarray.

It did not matter; she was my friend. I sometimes wonder if she lived to be tormented by her neuroses, but then I wonder as well, is it even possible for someone to have a Jewish girl for a friend and a Storm Trooper for a father in the same lifetime and not be tormented by neuroses?

In fact, our family theology seemed not too different from that of our neighbors. Like most of them, we made frequent references to a somewhat generic Dear God in Heaven who was said to be in control of the universe. I early took the signs of respect shown to that deity to be emblematic of social convention rather than of sincerely held belief since it made little sense for intelligent people to pay homage to what sounded like a white-bearded super-masculine divinity enthroned above the clouds who could make everything right but chose not to. I did not express my skepticism in this regard to others; people were shocked enough to learn that I did not believe in fairies.

Too timid to contradict my elders and too cynical to believe what they were teaching me, I became privately God-obsessed. I looked for proofs of God's existence everywhere. I threw out challenges to God to prove His existence to me: if you really are, then show me a sign and I will believe it! And then I lectured myself without mercy. What impudence! Do you think that you are smarter than Abraham, Isaac and Jacob, that you know more than they did? They could believe in God and you little know-it-all know better? Are you perhaps smarter than all the thousands of Jews who came before you, who were your ancestors? Don't you think they had the same doubts?

To these assertions I had no answers so I shamed myself into attending religious services with my parents without remonstrance and dutifully saying my Shema every night when I went to bed. As instructed, I asked God to bless me and my parents and grandparents. If my parents could act as if they believed what all other Jews seemed to want people to believe they believed, I would do likewise.

Shema Yisrael Adonai Elohenu Adonai Echad, I intoned nightly in Hebrew. The words seemed to comfort my mother and did no one any harm. Not only that, but I liked playing the role of the light-bearing servant.

≈ ≈ ≈

remembering and forgetting

KRISTALLNACHT

It was on November 9th of 1938 that everything changed. Although the date was soon to be indelibly burned into familial memory, the day slipped by uneventfully. I was almost eight and on vacation, a perpetual vacation, the Nazis having ruled out schooling for Jewish children. My mother and I were visiting my grandparents in the beautiful seaport city of Hamburg and having a good time with them as always, still living a normal life.

I was as happy as my nature allowed to be again among the wondrous sights and sounds of the big city, where I could walk along broad tree-lined avenues with my Opa Emil on our way to visit lush green parks or to stare in awe at endless numbers of gigantic ocean liners coming to dock at the busy port. When he took me into tiny bakeries wherein the air was thick with the aroma of freshly baked breads and cakes and bought me jelly-filled doughnuts with sugary coatings to eat when I should have been saving my appetite for dinner, it seemed the best of times.

I wanted to see everything, do everything, learn everything. Going out with my grandmother in the late afternoons offered special opportunities. Down the famed Grindelallee we would go, hand in hand, entering one specialty store after another to buy items for the evening's

remembering and forgetting

dinner. "We cannot buy these cucumbers," she said to me one day, passing on the oral tradition of vegetable selection. "I can see that they are all bitter and not worth our money."

Anyone who could see bitterness knew things I wanted to learn. I never strayed from her side; I clung to her every word, hoping she would reveal even greater mysteries. When she tucked me in gently under the giant eiderdown comforter and listened to me recite my Shema at night, it felt like the safest of times. November 9th was a day like that for us, one we did not have to remember because nothing special happened. At least, not to us. We did not know then that it was our last day of what passed for normal life.

Early the next morning, just as we were sitting down to breakfast, the first word came of the night's violent happenings. Friends and neighbors came to the apartment with whispered news that hundreds of Jewish men had been picked up on the streets and in their homes by the SS, the black-shirted storm troopers. There was hushed consternation at these reports. One could not say too much or speak too loudly. Even the appearance of criticism of the government was tantamount to treason and punishable as such. It was best to believe and to act as if the walls had ears. It was smarter not to give voice to the questions that, in any case, required no utterance: What was meant by these disappearances? What would happen to their men? What could be made of the rumors that synagogues were burning in Hamburg and in small towns here and there and that there was violence against Jewish owned property?

All knew better than to expect further information from the news media; there were no means of communication not totally controlled by the Nazis, who would reveal the day's events only when and if it suited them. The news, and the lack of news, made my mother nervous. She was anxious about the safety of my father who had stayed at

remembering and forgetting

home in Bünde to tend to business. She tried to call him by telephone.

"That number is not in service," the operator informed her. "There is no telephone at that house."

"There was a telephone there yesterday," my mother said. Now, fifty years later, she repeats the sentence in the same semi-timid, semi-assertive voice she used then. She is an actress with power.

"But not today." Cold, bureaucratic, final, is the inflection my mother uses. Clearly, the sentence said more to her than the import of its words. That voice, that voice that she recaptures now could have told her with-out quavering that my father was dead. Surely she thought he was dead when she heard it.

My mother responded to the operator's firmness by heading for the door, intending to take the next train back to Bünde. My grandmother put an end to that notion despite the strong instinct towards generosity that has been so idealized by her daughters that they boast even to this day, half a century after her death, of Oma's generous spirit, reminding me again how she once took all the money she had saved and scrimped to buy herself a warm new winter coat and then gave it to a woman who needed one more than she did and how, even in the concentration camp to which she was eventually trans-ported (as was learned from survivors who were there with her), she managed to contrive ways to help persons in greater distress than her own. All of which did not, of course, stop the Nazis from lining her up with hundreds of other poor souls forced to dig a mass grave in the frozen desolate soil outside of Minsk until it was large enough to hold them all, at which point the experienced sharpshooters needed only to shoot a few rounds before all were dead, or at least dying, in the hole they had created. That's the kind of efficiency the master plan called for.

remembering and forgetting

But now Oma had only advice to give. "Wait a moment, darling," she said. "You think that you can simply run off and leave me with a child to be responsible for? Or do you want to take her on what might well be a dangerous trip for the two of you? Who knows what waits for you out there? Stay here. You are safer in a big city than in that small village of yours where everybody knows everybody else. Stay here. We'll be safe together."

My mother stayed. What I could hear of Oma's words alternately upset and calmed me. I had been sent off to another room to play, to be out of hearing for the disturbing information that was floating about. It was better, safer, for children to know as little as possible. In a world in which children are expected to -- and do -- report their parents to civil authorities for even verbal infractions of the law, adults must be cautious.

("Oh, gosh. I don't remember what I felt then, whether I was scared or not," my mother says now when I try to delve into her emotions at the time. "You know I am not as complicated as you are. I guess I was nervous. I did not know what to think. I was not used to thinking for myself. Naturally it was worrisome that Daddy was not with us -- I worried even if he was five minutes late in coming home from work at night -- but you are the one who had to lie down with a cold washcloth on your head that night. If anyone was anxious, it was you.")

I can imagine myself quarantined in that little room off the kitchen, my ear to the door, straining to hear the frightening stories being shared in the parlor, feeling the anguish of those whose loved ones had disappeared on their way home from work or who had been publicly arrested without cause. Knowing what I know now about anxiety, I can break out in a cold sweat and re-agitate my heart to a violent pace just thinking about that little person, me, scared half to death all the while my mother was protecting,

remembering and forgetting

or trying to protect, me from disturbing news.

I can feel, as if for the first time, the terror, the sheer frightfulness that must have overcome me as I survived those moments alone but in fact I remember nothing, nothing. I don't remember being afraid then, or ever, which I take as strong evidence that my imaginings of those moments are true. So it is no wonder that I lay down, as my mother's account suggests, overcome with anxiety and quivering in fear-filled solitude until she came in and laid a cool cloth on my forehead and lent me the balm of her presence.

It was sometime later that same evening that my father's sister Hanna arrived with a breathless report that her fiancé had left for safety in Holland, slipping out the back door of his apartment as the SS broke down the front door to arrest him. He had not, in fact, found safety. Eventually, after they were married, he went with her to a concentration camp from which only she was released; he had been killed in some never detailed fashion. She knew how he died but never said. We asked but all we ever got in response was a frightful cynical smile. She came safely to the United States, tried to make a normal life for herself, and died fifty years later at the age of eighty-six, never having said a word to anyone about the horrors she had witnessed or the pain she had herself experienced.

But for this moment, she felt secure about his safety and the women were encouraged by his escape. One had to be hopeful. When evening came, she and my mother walked to the railroad station to meet the train coming in from Bünde on the slight chance that my father might be arriving on it. It was just a few blocks to the station. We always walked that distance; it was not worth taking the available streetcar. So the two women stood quietly, hopefully, on the street near the station, scrutinizing every passing man, knowing how dangerous it was for Jewish men, and maybe for them, to be out in public, when they saw a streetcar come by with -- what a wonderful, unexpected sight they saw -- my father hanging precariously on the outside step, the car so crowded that there was barely room for him on the platform.

He had, indeed, come in on the train and, not knowing what was going on in Hamburg, had chosen to hide himself in the crowd on the streetcar rather than walking the few blocks as he had always done before. My mother claims that it was that decision that saved his life but gives the credit to her guardian angel for leading him to make the decision that ensured his safety.

As it turned out, it was not his first escape of the day. He had risen early to make a short trip to a nearby town to consult a cousin just released from prison. He hoped that this cousin might provide him with information that would help him in rescuing his own brother, newly imprisoned for *Rassenschande*, racial shame, which is what the Nazis called the crime against the Race committed by a Jew who married a non-Jew.

So my father was not home when the trouble started in Bünde. When he returned and heard that Jews were being picked up and arrested, he ran quickly to a nearby Jewish residence which served as a center of Jewish communal life. He had barely begun to discuss the frightening news with the Levisons when SS men came and started ransacking the house before their startled eyes. Quietly, helplessly, they watched the storm troopers vandalize the family possessions, watched as crystal and china treasures were gleefully tossed against the walls.

My father had quickly seen enough. He moved softly toward the door, hoping to leave without being observed. An SS officer looked up from his plundering and yelled out to him, "Hey, Levison!" He was, you have to know, a small man, no more than five foot three or four and he looked

remembering and forgetting

very meek and unimposing, which may explain why he got away with what he did. He smiled and said, "No, Spiegel!" and managed to convey in those two words the crucial lifesaving message that he was the wrong person, a person nobody as important as this respected officer could possibly want to interrupt his important work to bother with, and kept moving.

He made his way home and prepared to leave for Hamburg. He now knew that Bünde was no longer safe for Jews. If any family should have been safe from violence, should have earned the protection of the city fathers, it was the wealthy Levison family, whose industry and generosity had filled city coffers for many years. Now they were being treated as criminals. "They had to bring in officers from other cities to do the plundering," my mother says now. "The local officials would never have done such a thing to the Levisons." My mother does not carry grudges.

My father looked around briefly. Getting away was suddenly urgent. He packed a few things, including a piece of butter -- butter was scarce and valuable but still he never could explain afterwards why he chose that of all things to carry with him -- and locked up the house and left. He headed for the train station, meaning to take the first train anywhere just to get out of town, to get lost in some limbo where he could not be found if the goons should decide to look for him, without stopping to think until he saw him that the station-master might stand in the way of his travels. The man's uniform jolted him back to reality. There was no point in going elsewhere, the man would remember his choice of destination. So he simply asked for a ticket to Hamburg and waited to see what would happen.

The stationmaster said, "They did not take you?"

"No, I was out of town," my father replied And that was it.

remembering and forgetting

"You see how lucky he was?" my mother asks as she tells me this story one more time. "The man knew your father to be a Jew, but it made no difference to him. He let him go." She takes it as proof of the goodness of man that the trainmaster sold him a ticket.

So my father got safely on the train and luckily off the train and caught the streetcar by sheer luck or inspiration and rode past my mother and aunt standing in the street. And to this day my mother feels certain that he was protected somehow, that her guardian angel was watching out for him hanging out there at the edge of the car where everybody could see him, where he could have been kicked off or pulled off, never to be seen again, so that somehow he was able and lucky enough to make it home safely to the apartment of my grandparents who hid him away, away from the light of the sun and the prying eyes of neighbors until he finally said that he could not stand it anymore, that he would turn himself in to the authorities rather than stay in hiding.

"Not a day goes by," my father said to me just before a careless surgical knife ended his life more than forty years later, "not a day goes by that I don't remember that day, and your grandparents, God rest their souls." He was habitually ruminative, intent on making sense of things. He had neither time nor reasoning power sufficient to make sense of the events of *Kristallnacht* and their immediate and ultimate consequences.

But he did come out into the sunlight again and, finding the atmosphere relatively calm, led us back to Bünde not knowing what we would find. To our grateful amazement, we had been spared again, had been lucky again, our possessions not so much destroyed as pawed over. The storm troopers that came to our residence had been interrupted in their pillage by the German citizen to whom my father had sold his business; he had boldly

remembering and forgetting

declared to the vandals that everything within the premises belonged to him, nothing to us.

This generous, risk-taking lie protected our belongings from destruction. Not long afterwards we were able to pack a few of those belongings and start on our voyage to America -- all of us together and totally unharmed. Lucky, lucky, lucky.

Sometimes I think that my mother must be right. She must have a guardian angel that watches over us. What else can explain our good fortune? Certainly one cannot thank God for such an anomaly. Who could imagine a God, who would even *want* a God that looks out for one family here and there while millions of others are decimated?

Not me.

Better to have no God at all.

≈≈≈

remembering and forgetting

MOVING ON

So we crossed the seas, made our way to the promised land and settled humbly into the small Chicago apartment of relatives who had preceded us, trying to stay out of their way while we stayed close enough to learn what we could from them, as if they had so quickly gained entrée to the American mystique. Glad to have our feet steady on land again, we were ready to move ahead with our new life and to put behind us everything we remembered about the old.

    We never stopped moving long enough to talk about the past, never even discussed the thirteen long days on the ship that carried us to America, thirteen days of stormy skies and churning water in which the vessel listed and tilted enough to keep my mother seasick from one edge of the ocean to the other so that I was on my own, free and unattended to explore and wander and wonder alone. Somehow I was expected to forget the variety and intensity of that experience, forget trying to impress the grown-ups with my precocious sensibilities, forget eating my meals alone in the vessel's massive dining hall while my father catered to my mother's needs, forget the aroma of the tea with lemon which pervaded my mother's cabin and which, still today, acts as an olfactory stimulant to subconscious nostalgia.

Perhaps if we had stopped our forward march long enough to talk about the journey, it would have occurred to me sooner, sooner than now, this moment, that my mother was not seasick at all even though that was what she always said in relating her memories of the ocean voyage, even though it was what she believed, believes, to have been the case. But who knew about anxiety attacks back then? What woman would have admitted to such weakness in those days, which required so much strength? Certainly not my mother, even if she was only twenty-nine years old and barely accustomed to the harsh responsibilities of adulthood and parenthood when she was forced to say good-bye to her mother and father with the full awareness she was unlikely to see them ever again.

What my mother remembers now about the journey is that she was seasick, terribly seasick, and so nauseous (she is ashamed to admit this) that she allowed my father to buy her a drink of Cognac from the ship's bar in order to settle her queasy stomach, a double indulgence which even the passage of fifty years has not made more acceptable.

"We didn't have any money, you know," she tells me. "And the Germans only allowed us to take ten dollars out of the country, which wasn't very much with which to set up housekeeping for a family of three, even by 1939 standards, and we certainly did not have a penny to waste on liquor. But the worst part, and this is the irony that made me feel really so irresponsible, was that someone, a friend wishing us farewell and *bon voyage*, had brought us a gift bottle of Cognac before we left, and we had turned it down, believing it to be extra baggage for which we had no use. And then, when I felt so terrible, that was just what I wanted and we had to spend money for the very same thing!"

The guilt she felt, feels, for having been so extravagant as to buy an expensive drink to quell the nausea was

remembering and forgetting

nothing compared to the relief I felt on seeing that the drink made her feel strong enough to lift herself up off the bed and actually leave the cabin for the first and last time between the seaports that framed our lives, and also nothing compared to the gratitude I feel now, considering what good luck it was that she was thereafter able to maintain her equilibrium on land without further recourse to mood-altering agents.

But then again, maybe she really was just seasick. Who can know? She does not admit to such other weaknesses as might explain her malaise and the truth is that once she was on solid ground again, she was fine. She arranged a visit with the distant cousin who had assumed responsibility for our livelihood by signing the affidavits that made our timely emigration possible. He had money and principles.

He gave me a dollar to introduce me to George Washington, "the father of our country," he said, and while I was still wondering what that could possibly mean, he offered my mother a job on the assembly line of his perfume factory. She had never worked outside the home before but now she welcomed the opportunity to help make our family self-sufficient. My father quickly followed her into the job market with a job as a stock boy in a downtown department store where he earned eighteen dollars a week, before taxes. We were set.

It was mid-March of 1939 when we rented an apartment within our means, which is to say a small third-floor flat with one bedroom and a special sleeping area designated for me in a curtained foldaway bed in the dining room. There was not an inch to spare but the flat established our identities as Chicago residents, and we quickly marched ourselves to the neighborhood school to take advantage of its benefits. I was eager to resume my interrupted education, to learn the strange language I had

remembering and forgetting

to master if I was ever to communicate my thoughts to anyone other than my parents. To the briskly efficient principal, I was an administrative problem of a new sort. After a brief interrogation and a look at my last and to him totally indecipherable German report card, he decided that kindergarten was the place for me to start. The facts supported his judgment.

My English language skills were primitive, my vocabulary basically still restricted to the few English words my parents had imparted to me from their somewhat more expansive repertoire, words like "cheese" and "table" and "chair"and "please" and "thank you", supplemented by the useful words I had been taught by the neighborhood children: "shaddup" and "getaddahere". But the word "kindergarten" was German and I expressed my indignation at the proposed humiliation. I was eight years old and kindergarten was for children.

To his credit, the administrator of Humboldt Elementary School, who in 1939 had no prior experience with immigrant children and the possibility of their special needs, nonetheless had the sensitivity to yield to my instincts. He allowed me to start my American education in the first grade, where the fictional Dick and Jane became my first and for a long time only friends. Run, Dick, run. See Jane run. See Dick and Jane run.

Compared to the rigor of the German classroom, the classwork soon struck me as an intellectual debasement. The reading material, though written in a new and unruly language, was embarrassingly simple-minded. I imagined it to be embarrassing for the other students as well to read such inane material but I did not dare to ask if that was so. I was sure they saw me as just another child who had moved into the neighborhood at the wrong time of year, inconsiderate of school calendars and undeserving of too much attention.

≈42≈

remembering and forgetting

With my immigrant's clothing and my limited and accented English, my classmates seemed to find me alien enough to be peculiar. What was worse, they thought I was German and I had neither the inclination nor the language skills needed to explain why I did not think of myself as German. I was a child without a country. I could not explain that to myself.

And whom could I ask about such problems? My parents were both tired at the end of their long workdays, my little father sore and fatigued from tackling and moving oversized boxes of merchandise from one floor to another, my mother frazzled from assembling perfume packages in a factory where the production schedules were maintained with a rallying imperative of "More speed, girls! let's keep it moving, girls!" I was little disposed to burden them with my existential concerns. They did their jobs. I knew mine: to learn the language, to take care of myself, to become an American.

And to forget the past. That was the most important thing, to keep moving forward, and not to get mired down in the whirlpool we had left behind us. I did the best I could, learning and forgetting, as fast as was in my power.

≈ ≈ ≈

remembering and forgetting

.GETTING TOUGH

The water ran hot on my feet, much too hot for comfort but that was all right. It was what I wanted. I was prepared to have it even hotter. I turned the faucet a fraction of an inch further and tested the increased temperature with one foot raised into the stream. It was hot, hot, hot, but I could take it. For a while, I could take it.

I steeled myself for the pain I would feel as the intense heat spread throughout the tub. It was part of my plan to use my nightly bath as an opportunity to desensitize myself incrementally so that one day I would be able to sit in a tubful of scalding water and not cry out in pain. I aimed to make myself so heroically tough that I would bravely hold my tongue no matter what I was forced to endure. I was trying to build a veneer of stoicism on which I could rely if push ever came to shove, if unpredictable fate were ever to bring me, after all, face to face with the kind of harsh treatment I would certainly have encountered in Germany had we not been so lucky as to get out in the nick of time. I hoped at the very least to deny any prospective torturers whatever perverse satisfaction they hoped to get out of torturing me. I wanted to be strong in the face of any threat.

remembering and forgetting

It irritated me that the process was so slow and I was so weak. Every day I tried raising the temperature an iota more but made only the slightest progress in tolerating the increased discomfort. I saw little hope of ever pushing my pain threshold high enough to survive the kind of cruelties that were the daily fare in the concentration camps in which my relatives were interred. Not that I really expected anything like that to happen to me. We were safe from all that, I was sure. Still, how can one ever be sure? Were not the Jews in Germany sure nothing would happen to them?

I could not bear thinking about how those poor people were suffering. How could they stand it? How could anyone stand such suffering? such pain? I knew that I could not hold out, that I would fall apart at the first blow. I had to toughen myself, just in case. I did not want to make a fool of myself or embarrass my parents with my infantile fearfulness. I made the water just a little hotter and told myself, as my mother kept reminding me, how lucky we were to be safe, how easy life was for me, now that we were in America.

I examined my fingers. They looked thoroughly wrinkled from the exposure to the hot water but not at all charred. Good. I was holding them longer and longer in the flame of the Sabbath candle without feeling the pain and without really burning myself. Perhaps my body was actually getting tougher. My mind, well, that was another question; it was completely out of control. I was always afraid. With my mother off to work every day, I was alone for many hours every day, allowing more time than I needed to anticipate danger.

My only defensive technique consisted of running., as fast as I could, away from danger. Like the day I lost my way trying to find the new school I was supposed to start after we moved to the new apartment. My mother had shown me the way I was supposed to go but I took the wrong turn somewhere and was already in a frenzy of fear as I ran down one block after another, afraid to stop and ask anybody where I was, when two boys much bigger than I who were sitting on the front stoop of their house, watching the world go by and looking for trouble, yelled at me, Run, you dirty Jew, run. The words had set my head afire. This sort of thing was not supposed to happen. My parents had told me that Jews were safe in America!

Run, Jew, run! they had shouted after me, and I had run. I had run without stopping to breathe until I turned a corner and saw the school before me, a sure haven of refuge. Sprinting up to the massive doors, I had felt my heart racing and my hands cold with sweat. I knew that I had never been more frightened in my life and the realization shamed me. No one had laid a hand on me; I had been in no real danger whatsoever. There was no excuse for being so afraid when nothing bad had happened to me. It was ridiculous to be so afraid when I was altogether safe.

Safe as I was in my own bathtub, where I could think rationally, where it was perfectly clear that heightened ability to withstand pain would be an asset. Just in case. I carefully lowered my chest into the hot water, compressing my lips so that no moan would escape to betray my distress.

≈ ≈ ≈

remembering and forgetting

A GOOD GIRL

I want to be fair about this. I don't want to give my childhood a bad rap by selective memories that suggest I wallowed in misery every day, when the truth is that I was just a good little girl who went to school gladly and enjoyed studying and learning as well as the approval that my good grades earned. At least. now and then. "Just a B in gym?" my father joked whenever I came home with a report card. "Is that the best you can do?"

He did not mean to hurt me with his kidding, I was sure. He had to know that it was indeed the best I could do since I was totally uncoordinated and not any better at athletics than he was, although he may not ever have known exactly how frightening a softball can be when it is flying through the air at your head, and how embarrassing it is when you cannot stop yourself from ducking. He didn't grow up in baseball country and probably never had to learn for himself that getting a B in physical education was harder than getting A's in academic classes.

By the age of ten, I was fully on my own, doing to the best of my ability what my parents expected me to be doing. I kept myself busy after school with books and chores my mother left for me when she went off to work. I peeled potatoes for supper. I bought minor grocery items from the

remembering and forgetting

neighborhood store. I did my homework. And I visited a generous neighbor who allowed me to care for her baby without ever making me aware that she was caring for me. Every day, I was welcome to come and do whatever I could to keep the baby amused, labor for which I was compensated in cookies and kindness. This daily opportunity left little time for making friends closer to my age, which was just fine with me. I felt too different from the other Chicago fifth-graders to require more of their company than I was privy to during the school day.

    I wished I could explain that to the grandparents we had left behind in Germany. They seemed to want me to become a social butterfly when, in fact, I had always been a serious child. They should have remembered that, even if they never received the long letters I wrote them to keep them apprised of my activities. The letters we received from them were few. I still hold the last one that came to me from Hamburg late in 1941, shortly before their deportation to Hell. It is written on the back of an instruction form for people wishing to immigrate to the United States; all the blank areas surrounding the instructions have been cut out in the interest of weight-reduction so that the paper has a jagged, irregular edge. Since the printed information itself is undisturbed, I take it to have been no random choice of writing paper. It was too late, much too late then to think of emigration.

    This is what my grandmother wrote to me when I was ten:

My sweet Mirjam!

> I believe that you have totally forgotten your Omi and Opa. I have written you so often but you have never answered. What do you do all day? How many girlfriends do you really have? And which classroom do you honor with your little persona? I mean, in the way we are used to knowing you.

remembering and forgetting

My sweet Mirjam, it is very nice for you to read good books but you must also play with your schoolmates. One is soon enough grown up so that playtime is over and done with. Then one would often be glad to play and be happy to return to one's childhood again.

Do you know what Opa says every morning?
'Soon I'll be able to go through Chicago with my Mirjam, she'll show us everything beautiful then & I will eat chocolate and ice cream with Mirjam forever. That will be a glorious life.' Best of all, he would like to buy all of Hamburg for you! But then he always asks, 'Do you think that Mirjam still prays for us the way she always used to do here? The dear God always fulfills the prayers of good little children!'

So my beloved Mirjam, stay always a good girl. Kisses from the heart from

Your Oma and Opa

Of course, I stayed a good girl. Always. I never thought of being otherwise and, besides, what choice did I really have, when so much depended on my being good? I mean, imagine me, ten years old, reading this letter and recognizing the import of my grandparents' faith: God would spare them if I would only do my part!

Yes, yes, yes, Oma, Opa. You can bet your Goddamned lives I will be good.

≈≈≈

remembering and forgetting

ADAPTATIONS

Practical child that I was, I never wanted anything that I did not have, never yearned for anything beyond my reach, except for this, this one transcending fantasy: at eleven I wanted to be like Brenda Starr, the beautiful, intelligent heroine of my favorite comic strip in the daily paper. In those days, Brenda was the orphaned daughter of a brilliant research scientist who had made it possible before his untimely demise for her to simply press a tiny spot on the underside of her wrist in order to become instantaneously and monumentally invisible. What a rare and precious gift this was!

The beautiful Brenda, whose glorious curls I also envied, was able to insinuate herself into any place and any situation that piqued her curiosity, watching and listening her fill as events unfolded. This incredible knack of hers gave her a fantastic professional advantage over her rivals (she was a newspaper reporter like Lois Lane, but prettier, smarter!) and allowed her to throw terror into the hearts of wrongdoers by reincarnating herself in the midst of their conspiratorial huddles by pressing her finger on her wrist once more.

remembering and forgetting

What I would not have given for such amazing talent! Merely imagining myself able to travel unseen, slipping in and out of private and forbidden settings wherein I could observe without being observed and overhear without detection what was being said about anything, but especially about me, gave me a vision of heaven on earth. I half believed and altogether hoped that I had my own invisibility pressure point that my surreptitious searches would one day uncover, after which I would wander the world free from observation, free from derisive laughter, free from the need to conform to the expectations of others.

Coming in late to being an American child was proving onerous. The others knew things I could not seem to learn and no one could teach me. Learning the language had been easy enough. I simply gave up speaking German and dove into my new medium of communication with such zeal and fervor that it was only a matter of a few short months before I was fully able to communicate with the native inhabitants of my small world. It took a little longer to rid myself of my Germanic intonations, to teach my tongue the gentle twists and turns that would allow my consonants to become soft enough so that the neighborhood baker would no longer smile in amusement at my requests for the only alternative to soft, doughy textureless American breads that we had discovered. "I vant a rrrrye brrrread from yesterrr-day," I would say, handing over the nickel clutched in my hand and blushing with the awareness that I was rolling my r's and hardening my v's in very un-American fashion. Repeating the phrase now makes me feel like an immigrant again.

In any case, it wasn't the language that stood in my way. It was me. I was too serious, too intent on my studies, too preoccupied with my differences from everyone else. I worried too much about getting things right, about following the rules. I laughed only with premeditation, usually after an observation that others were laughing and

remembering and forgetting

the concomitant assumption that something I did not understand was amusing and merited laughter.

The worst part was that I knew all this. Self-consciously, I saw myself not behaving properly, not looking right. I practiced facial expressions in front of the bathroom mirror, trying to look as happy and carefree as my classmates. Judging my reflection carefully, I would force my facial muscles into a wide variety of smiles, trying to find one that fit. I would open my eyes wide and try closing them seductively, fluttering eye-lashes flirtatiously at my image, while I looked in the glass for the American me. I picked a wide-eyed innocent look with a cheerful smile but away from the mirror I lost it.

Away from the mirror, in the real world of the school yard, I tried out the rehearsed smiles while I watched the others play their games. None of them felt right to me. I wanted to melt into the background, to get lost, before the teacher asked me, again, to go play with the other kids. Although my arms soon showed the bruises that were the only product of my persistent searches for the pressure point that would render me undetectable, I never found it. Regretfully, I accepted my visibility.

≈≈≈

<u>remembering and forgetting</u>

AN ORDINARY DAY

I put my childhood behind me, married the first decent man that was willing to gamble on me, and busied myself with doing. More or less successfully, I put an end to introspection until one ordinary September day, as such days are measured by those who are trained to assess the passing days in terms of temperature gradients, barometric pressures, heat indices and measurable precipitation, my entire defenses crumbled.

The day did not seem ordinary to me as I stood at the door, head aching, blood throbbing violently through suddenly narrowed channels, staring out through the space I had opened between the front door and its frame. I looked around and slowly raised my eyes to check for rain, or better, for signs of imminent danger. No such luck, there was no sign of storm. The blue sky only felt gray. The massive clouds that seemed to filter the sunlight from view were wholly invisible to the eye. He'll have to go, I thought. He'll go and everything will be all right and he will come back.

"It's time," I said, and clutched his hand, then let him go. I watched him crossing the street carefully. A dull leaden weight was settling into my belly. He turned and for a fraction of a second I saw on his small face the half-smile my father used to smile when he wanted to impress me as wholly wise and mature and appeared, instead, as engagingly boyish. A moment later, having reached the other side of the street, the child turned away from me again and, abandoning caution, flew up the hill and out of sight. He knew the way. There was no need to worry.

I stayed at the door, staring still at the path his feet had traced a moment ago. I forced a smile at my own reflection in the glass. How innocent, how precious he looked, the last of my brood to tumble out of the nest and away from my hovering attentions. He was ready for solo flights, no doubt about that in his mind at all while I, I had enough doubts for all of them, enough for generations of descendants.

I turned away from the door. He was gone and, just as quickly, it was overwhelmingly clear to me: my usefulness was over, there was nothing left in life for me. My children were growing up and did not need me anymore. Nobody needed me. What was I to do?

Reflexively, I slapped myself in the face with cold reason. There was no excuse for my feeling so desolated by the most ordinary developmental phase, the need to send a child off to start kindergarten. It was ridiculous, too ridiculous for words, to feel so devastated, almost as if I were depressed, as if a rational woman with a perfectly honorable husband and three wonderful children -- all healthy and happy -- could get depressed on such a minor pretext.

Rationally, I pushed the glumness aside. It was a momentary psychological aberration, a simple hormonal imbalance, a weird astrological confluence, a normal phase of the moon that would pass. I tried coaxing my lips into another smile but had forgotten which muscles to use. The effort was too demanding, the semblance of optimism suddenly beyond my reach. It was embarrassing, this inability to achieve a facade of composure. I shook my head in frustration and anger as if the agitation would improve its functioning in the same way we some-times try to revive appliances falling out of our control.

    Enough, enough, I thought, forcing myself to action. I put the breakfast dishes into the sink and washed them with a clatter. The house was too quiet, despite the jocularity coming over the airwaves. Arthur Godfrey harassing Julius La Rosa failed to amuse. I had not been so alone in ten years, not since the first child was born. Here at last was the quiet time for myself that I had often longed for when all the demanding voices cried for my attention and I was spoiling it with my unreasonable gloominess. I put my head down on the newly wiped breakfast table, my fingers tracing the pattern of abstract skylarks on the laminated plastic tabletop. Rivulets of tears flowed artfully among the jagged lines. Oh, God, I cried out to myself, when I am finished counting all the bird shapes on the tabletop, then what am I to do? Wait for the children all day even though they could take care of themselves if they had to, and might even be better off if they did?

    Am I nothing now but mother?

    Like the letters on a Ouija board, the tears on the table spelled out the truth. I was unfit for anything. My education had left me unprepared for the humdrum existence in which I was caught up. None of the excellence for which I had striven in college was transferable to this arena. No matter how hard I worked, my house was never clean enough, my mothering never good enough, my manner never pleasant enough to suit me. Always, with a restless third eye, I watched myself failing in my attempts to master the daily routines that were too simple-minded to justify discussion, too necessary to permit complaint.

remembering and forgetting

I was stuck in a trap of my own making and had no honorable way out. Surely, the human race could not have survived the myriad difficulties of its existence if women had not long ago taken on and willingly shouldered the burdens of homemaking with good grace. It was a fair enough social contract with a price that seemed not at all excessive, even in current market terms. Smarter women than I had been living the same restricted lives for millennia, I knew. I saw no valid reason for complaint, no solid basis for unhappiness; I was lucky merely to be alive and should, by all rights, be grateful to live my life in the apparently unthinking way other women seemed to employ. Why could I not figure out how they managed to do that?

The difficulty sprang from having to while away the hours not occupied by child and husband care. While other women were content enough to have some time for themselves, happy enough to wander through the stores to shop for necessities or even for glamorous garments to store away for the wonderful occasions that inevitably ended any temporary doldrums that came along, I found no pleasure in such unstructured activities. They allowed too many opportunities for thought. Thinking interfered with living, I found, rephrasing the Cartesian credo to my own truth: I think, therefore, I am not.

It was easier to do the hard work, the scrubbing and cleaning and child-tending chores that multiplied so readily, than to permit the spontaneous generation of the hard questions I could not answer: was this the best I could do with my life? killing time between the regimented mealtimes? between the needs of one or another family member? was it for this that I was saved?

But it was precisely not knowing why I was saved that had made it easy to give up college for marriage, as if the time-sanctioned use of woman's time would prove its value in the doing better than it ever could in theory.

remembering and forgetting

L'appetit vient en mangeant, my mother used to say whenever I claimed to have no appetite for a meal and the wisdom of that saying had persuaded me that I might acquire a taste for marriage once I tried it. The prospect of doing something, anything, useful was in any case so irresistible that, lacking any clear-cut plan or any vision for a meaningful existence that I had to surrender, I had seized the opportunity to fall into someone else's life plan. At the least, making one other person happy would be a worthwhile accomplishment.

Marriage had kept me busy, had let me stop think-ing about what I could do with my life, how I could make the world a better place. I only had to take each day as it came and to push the questions out of mind. And it had worked, for better or for worse, until now. Until I watched that child go up the hill towards school, knowing even at five where he was going and how to get there. How different from me he was.

I put myself to bed to ponder my uselessness until it was time to greet the children with milk and cookies after school. I had been an actress. I could still act for an audience, act the role of loving devoted mother. When the first cheerful hello sounded at the door, I found a smile I had not used and saved the tears for another day.

That's one thing about tears: they keep for a really long time.

≈≈≈

remembering and forgetting

IN LIEU OF KADDISH

For eternal remembrance, there are inscribed in this book the names of 6000 Hamburg Jews, who as innocent sacrifices to National Socialist persecution, suffered death by force. May the names of these dead warn the living of all times never again to disregard the precepts of humanity and reverence for human life.

SENATE / HAMBURG 1965

It was 1983, years after the end of the war and the reshaping of the world into new configurations, that the first official word regarding the fate of my maternal grandparents reached us by means of the book that bears this dedication. It came in the mail, a belated gift from the City of Hamburg to all the involuntary expatriates on the city rolls, a symbolic representation of the changed political climate that the passage of time had wrought. The compassionate words hint at the possibility that even the worst evil can give birth to an iota of goodness, that a record of a world gone mad can serve as an incentive to future sanity, but such cheerful thoughts fade quickly as one confronts the somber facts collected in this volume.

It is fortunate for seekers after family lore that

remembering and forgetting

Germans are compulsively methodical. They keep good records as if by instinct, a fact relied on by the law-makers of Hamburg when they decided -- decades after the fall of the Hitler regime, when most Germans wanted nothing more than to forget the past, or at the very least, to minimize past horrors that were besmirching their innocent reputations -- to publish and disseminate the lists kept by their predecessors to record the names of all the Jews sent to their deaths under their terms of office.

The Table of Contents of the resulting memorial book, employing the same propensity for order by which millions were neatly exterminated and eliminated, tells the story in the sparsest of terms.

It begins like this:

REPORT ON THE DEPORTATION MEASURES
OF THE SECRET STATE POLICE IN HAMBURG
by Dr. Max Plaut,
Chairman of the Jewish Community
in Hamburg 1938 - 1943

The deportation transports

Transport to Lodz on October 25, 1941	1,034
Transport to Minsk on November 8, 1941	968
Transport to Minsk on November 18, 1941	407
Transport to Riga on December 6, 1941	753
Transport to Auschwitz on July 11, 1942	300

And so on and so on the listing goes, pointing the reader to the pages of vital statistics regarding the individuals hustled off to their deaths in each of the eighteen recorded shipments. By then current estimates, the deaths of eight thousand former Jewish citizens of Hamburg are

remembering and forgetting

directly attributable to Nazi brutality. So the assimilated head of the Jewish community put his own Germanic predilections for precision to good use in keeping book on the more than six thousand of his compatriots about whose fate he was informed. His careful records made possible the citations in these memorial pages, the only tombstones ever to commemorate the coming into and going from life of these doomed human beings. It serves no purpose to wonder if there was more that he could have done for the six thousand; we know better.

My grandparents, I learned from this volume, were in the second transport from Hamburg, very early in the implementation of the Final Solution; the Table of Con-tents shows that the Germans had to ship 14 pages full of people across East Germany and all of Poland to an execution site in Minsk because the more conveniently located death camps were not ready for the killing as soon as the killers were. I am confident that my grand-parents would have expressed sympathy for Max Plaut's role in the drama. Great respecters of authority, they would have been quick to jump to his defense, had there been, in the crowded cattle cars that shuttled them to their deaths in Minsk, any anarchists brazen enough to suggest that Jews should not cooperate in the displacement of Jews. They would have argued for the incontrovertible need for leadership within the community. One had to have faith in someone, they would have said, since God appeared unresponsive to their prayers.

And they would have been right. Plaut survived at least long enough to tell the tale. Such as it was.

His report starts late, three years to the day after the events of Kristallnacht made violence against the Jews a civic obligation of the highest order. My grand-father had been ready ever since, having packed his overnight bag with his travel necessities on the morning after

remembering and forgetting

Kristallnacht and kept it by the door, so that he could go with a semblance of dignity when the time came to be hauled away; whether or not he packed the Iron Cross earned for his military service to the Kaiser and the Fatherland was not recorded.

According to the Plaut account, the first hint of the imminent evacuations came on the 15th of October 1941, when word came by way of the Jewish community in Cologne that 20,000 Jews would be evacuated from Germany to Litzmannstadt (Lodz) during the month of October. A follow-up inquiry to the Hamburg Gestapo brought him the reassuring news: "Here there is nothing ordered."

Only ten days after that conversation, the first transport of Jews left from Hamburg. For this and each succeeding shipment, Plaut records the Nazi orders: who must go and who may stay, what they are allowed to pack, when and where they must present themselves, and to whom they must turn over the keys to their homes. He offers a dispassionate account, a mundane litany of routineness, a stereotypical example of assimilated Jewish homage to Germanic efficiency, ending with a modest expression of civic pride in the humanity displayed by those in charge of the deportations from Hamburg. "Only once," Plaut says in his concluding paragraph, "only once, with respect to a Transport to Minsk, did an accompanying officer of the Hamburg Security Police mishandle a transport participant so forcefully that he almost died."

Would he have been as composed, as cool, as detached, I wonder, if it had been his relatives who were among those chosen to be "participants" of this or any transport? But, then again, under the controlled Germanic facade, who knows what torments Plaut himself suffered, or what his own final fate would be? I try not to judge. One cannot pass judgment on all the good souls caught up in the

≈61≈

remembering and forgetting

maze of evil.

He was only the record keeper who made it possible for us to know the Final Destination that the German State arranged for my grandparents, whose names I list here, precisely as the City of Hamburg did on page 21 of its memorial book (along with the names of all those deported from Hamburg to Minsk on November 8, 1941), except that I do it with love and such prayer as my heart can muster:

Emil Josephi, 7.2.1881;
Frieda Josephi, nee Oppenheim, 12.9.1883

May the source of peace grant everlasting peace to their tormented souls and to the souls of all who still struggle with the knowledge of what happened -- there, to them, and to all of us, forevermore.

≈≈≈

remembering and forgetting

FORGETTING

Almost fifty years after Kristallnacht, I went back to revisit the scene of that crime. With my mother. When she first asked me whether I would like to join her on a trip to Hamburg, my heart skipped a beat. Go back to Germany? and revive the painful memories I had been suppressing so long?

All the fears of my fearful childhood roused themselves from slumber and contended for expression. I cannot do this, I thought. I will go crazy. My feet will step on German soil and I will lose whatever tenuous hold I have on sanity and go screaming like a Banshee through the streets, wailing against the past which I will misapprehend as a magically preventable future. Don't let it happen, I will be shouting as men in crisp uniforms keep marching towards me guns at the ready so that they can restrain me and enforce the civil order.

In my head, now feverishly hot and ready to explode into primal bursts of neurotic energy, I could already hear the chorus of inchoate shrieks I expected to be unable to hold back. I will fall apart and will never get the fragments of my being back together again into a cohesive whole. I will be a helpless child again, afraid of death and untold mortifications again. I will embarrass my mother, upset her

remembering and forgetting

no end. But if she can do this, how can I not? She is the one who lost her parents, not I. Perhaps this is required of me, something I must do, must prove to myself I can do. Rationally, in the way I always make decisions, I decided that making the trip while my mother was alive to accompany me was the right thing to do.

"Do you know?" my mother said to me much later, after we had come back largely unchanged, "do you know, when you first said that you were not sure you could face going to Germany, that I did not know what you meant? I thought, 'Germany is such a beautiful country, why would she not want to go there?'" My mother was telling me -- can you believe this? -- that she had for a time forgotten what happened in Germany. She is even better than I at forgetting. It is a skill one can obviously develop with practice and she has had lots of practice.

As it turned out, she was right to be unafraid. We saw nothing in Germany to be scared of, nothing reminiscent of the terror that we did not bring along our-selves. Hamburg, still one of the most beautiful cities in the world, shows no scars, no evidence of its participation in the dark business of the War Against the Jews. It looks less guilty of crimes against humanity than do Washington, D.C., New York City, or even St. Louis. It was easy for us to fall into the admiring tourist's role as we visited the cultural sites, toured the magnificent harbor, and wandered through the old and amazingly still familiar paths in the Botanical Garden. We managed to handle even City Hall (where all sorts of oppressive regulations had been efficiently and dutifully laid down, in their time) as civilized visitors to the city.

My mother enjoyed pointing out the familiar sights. And I, to my surprise, did not scream, not even once, not even when we walked on the old Grindelallee to the street on which the family had lived, not even when we stood in

remembering and forgetting

front of the apartment building at Durchschnitt #8. Like ordinary tourists, we expressed wonder that the building still stood, looking much as it had fifty years before, no older, no less habitable. And, look, there is the corner grocer I used to run to in order to buy a forgotten food item for my grandmother's table, still there, still standing. Was there a war? was there a Holocaust?

One could wonder. It was a peaceful scene, utterly devoid of harsh reminders of the hard years, and we, we were glad to just replay some old familial history, as if we were simply revisiting the residence of some unknown ancestors we had heard about who had lived at this site and who had died in their beds. So happy was I not to be screaming, not to be reminded by any visual clues of what had happened to my grandparents right in that very spot, not to mention what happened after, after they were deported in cattle cars across half of Europe, only to be shot and pushed into mass graves they had themselves been forced to dig, that I made no attempt to visit the actual apartment in which they were living when all this started.

Standing on the street in front of that building, concerned more about surviving what I already knew than acquiring new information, I followed my mother's lead in remembering the pleasant times we had enjoyed in my grandparents' apartment. I marveled at the stories my mother could tell about what went on there and at the stories she had forgotten.

"Why do you want to keep thinking about all this?" my mother asked me after we came back from our trip and I told her that I was writing something about the Holocaust. She seemed surprised, thinking perhaps that not talking about it one time during our trip would have killed that topic once and for all. "What good does it do anybody?" I don't know, I said, and that is the truth.

Is it better to remember or to forget?

remembering and forgetting

I don't know that either but imagine it to be the question Hamlet would have come to ponder, had he chosen to live and to contemplate the best way to put his sadness behind him.

Is it better to remember or to forget? Though rarely asked because we think we know the answer, it may be the most important question of our time. Is it better, as individuals and as a society, to recall and to pass on to generations yet to come the awful truths that we were forced to learn when human beings committed the most horrendous crimes ever imagined against other human beings? Survivors of the Holocaust spent forty mute years trying to resolve the tension between the conventional wisdom that it is important to remember and the instinctive knowledge that forgetting is the key to survival.

Forget, forget, forget, said the voices in their heads. Forget me, forget them, forget what happened, don't think about it. Get on with your life. Start over. Put it all behind you. Forget, forget, forget. Don't talk about it. Nobody can believe you. You are wasting your time. It is too awful for words. Put it away, away, away, deeper, deeper, deeper down. Forget it all.

But society said remember and, as if by mutual consent, after forty years in the wilderness of trying to forget and failing, survivors started telling their searing accounts of what, in fact, they had survived. And now that the world knows all about the horror, now that all the awful stories have been told, all the documentary films made and seen, all the Germans' own meticulous reports of the killings read and analyzed, and all the monuments in stone and film constructed or at least drafted, now the world is ready to remember.

To what end, I ask, echoing my mother. What good does it do? Are people made better by the knowledge of the depravity to which human beings can sink? Is this

remembering and forgetting

knowledge worth having, worth passing on? Are the well-intentioned people who declaim "Never Again" better able to defend against a recurrence of wholesale brutality against them or any people than the original victims of the Holocaust were? If there is a lesson to be learned from the Holocaust, I suspect it is a lesson not for you and not for me and certainly not for our children, but for the brutes who will not be persuaded to learn it and who cannot be restrained from defying it.

"Forget it," my mother says. "Get on with your life."

I would if I could.

≈

≈≈

remembering and forgetting

CALM NIGHTS

I do not sleep well. I put myself to bed with as much care and ritual as I would use for a colicky baby that needs its rest but what success I have is rare and intermittent. Although totally exhausted when I lie down, sleep remains steadfastly beyond my reach. I may have endless trouble keeping my eyes open while reading a book I very much want to read but the moment my head hits the pillow, I am wide awake, my systems irreversibly set at go. I know no way to turn my internal motor off.

I count sheep. I cool my brain. I raise barriers to thought and try to keep myself in a relaxation pose. I try not to think about sleeping, not to panic about not sleep-ing. It never works; my heart beats too loudly. The breathing of my partner is too heavy; the sound interferes with my concentration on my own deep breathing. I tell myself it does not matter, that we don't need as much sleep as we think we need. But I get hot and cold and more and more anxious although I don't allow it, won't let myself get anxious about not sleeping.

I wait for morning without any expectation that it will come. I keep track of the time with my eyes closed, feeling the hours pass, one by one. I need no other timepiece. I fall in and out of hasty snatches of sleep from which I waken

remembering and forgetting

roughly, as if by an earth tremor. By sheer force of will, I keep my body still, my breathing slow and measured, as I resist the forces pulling me into the whirling chaos that seems to surround me. I stay calm, motionless, determined not to yield to the fierce power of storms of my own making. I keep my eyes closed, simulating sleep, willing myself into restfulness, until morning comes.

At dawn I know before ever I open my eyes that it is too early to rise and that I will lose even the semblance of sleep if I move the smallest muscle. With mathematical conceits I try to spin an insulating shelter over the inert body I inhabit. In a courtyard visible only to my inner eye, I construct walls of cubic blocks reflecting the relationships between integers and the sets of square and odd numbers but barely manage to square fifteen before I break out in a cold sweat and give up.

I need something to help me sleep but my doctors don't trust me. It is frustrating, insulting, that they do not believe me. I would never kill myself, I have said more than once and they should believe me because I do not lie. I always tell the truth as well as I know it. I would never take my own life, although I have the greatest of sympathy for people who do. I understand the pain that seems to have no end, that takes all pleasure out of living, that taints all possible tomorrows with the certainty of endless misery, that stretches out the present instant of agony until it encompasses all time, past and future, until there is nothing, nothing but emptiness and sorrow.

I understand why people might want to put an end to their despair and how they may actually think for the moment in which the fatal decision is made that it is for the benefit of their loved ones that they intend to die, that killing themselves will materially improve the quality of life for their survivors by removing the vicarious suffering that their own misery causes.

remembering and forgetting

They are wrong, of course. Suicides create more sadness than is anticipated and often set a familial precedent that eventually becomes compelling to someone else. That alone is not a prospect I could face from the other side, looking back to see that I have made my survivors more miserable through an act of will than I ever did through all the unwilled errors of my life. In any case, killing oneself is not the kind of example one wants to set for family members whereas living with despair is at least morally instructive to others, and at most, clearly essential for the sort of spiritual enlightenment that would make living more tolerable.

So it is quite true that I would never kill myself and that it would be altogether safe (not to mention an act of humanity) to prescribe sedatives for me to give me some rest, to make life a little easier, to provide me with some break in the rhythm of desolate days and desperate nights, in the course of which I occasionally think that it would not be any great loss to wake up dead one morning. Not by my own hand. Just dead.

It is a great and tiring burden to be saved as once I was. To have to justify one's existence to oneself. To not be able to. And to have to keep trying, day after day, night after night. The consequence is a chronic anxiety that can keep a person up nights. It has been suggested to me by experts in these matters that I could sleep if I wanted to, that it is I myself that keep myself from sleeping, barring my unconscious deliberations through an exercise of excessive control.

To me it seems otherwise, that, in fact, I have so little control over my world that I am in a constant state of panic that I might lose the little control I have, leaving me suddenly unglued, splintered into all the various warring elements I try to hold together.

Of course, I would sleep if I could. There is nothing I

<u>*remembering and forgetting*</u>

would rather do than sleep. Peacefully. Endlessly.   Forever. But I will settle for one night. One Ambien.

≈≈≈

remembering and forgetting

GETTING RELIGION

Despite everything, I belong to a synagogue. I mean, I don't believe in God, and I don't believe organized religion has advanced humanity's progress as much as it has set it back but I still cannot cut the ancestral ties. It's something in the blood, I think, that requires the connection to continue, dormant though it may be. But when I decided on a whim to attend a Sabbath service one Saturday morning in July, I surprised myself. I have always stayed away from worship services; there was no reason to go that morning except that I had other business to do in the neighborhood and the idea had presented itself.

    I argued with myself, of course. On the one hand, I wanted to go, but on the other, the idea of my attending a prayer service seemed altogether ridiculous, an unnecessarily masochistic immersion in certain psychic alienation. Whenever I go to one of these services, the hypocrisy inherent in mouthing praises of a supposedly omnipotent God keeps me moodily silent and separate from those who find it perfectly natural to express such sentiments. I can never feel a sense of spiritual community with the fortunates who still believe in a cosmic force with the power

remembering and forgetting

to end suffering on earth, with people so out of touch with the harsh realities of this post-Auschwitz era that they can still give voice to the ancient summons to faith. So then I wonder what I am doing there.

But study is another matter, and the Torah study that follows the service was always somehow provocative, I reminded myself. I enjoy trying to make pragmatic, secular, everyday-living-kind-of sense out of the so-called holy literature. It could not hurt to go and sit quietly through the short worship service and then take part in the hour of intellectual stimulation that regularly follows.

When I arrived at the makeshift chapel, ten or twelve members were busily assembling the sanctuary: rearranging chairs, moving in the portable ark, carrying the Shabbat services in their stiff ring binders. The rabbi was catching up on the latest news in the lives of her congregants. I found a place in the circle of chairs and exchanged greetings with others. Our talented lay music leader started the service by strumming a song of peace on his guitar. As the others picked up the chant, I too joined in. *Sim, sim, sim shalom, sim, sim shalom.* I don't know why I was singing. It just seemed right. I wasn't even self-conscious about being unable to carry a tune. I had always said my singing was so bad that my children used to ask me please to keep quiet and let them sleep when I tried to sing lullabies to them, but that observation did not sound funny to me anymore. Whether I could sing or not did not seem to matter to anyone.

The rabbi started the service in a friendly, informal fashion. She had personal anecdotes to share first, then a few moments of inspiration aimed at breathing life into the old prayers. I felt immune to the tricks of her trade but found myself playing along, reading and chanting the Hebrew words to the best of my ability, avoiding the phonetic transliterations in the hope of improving my skills

remembering and forgetting

by concentrating on the original Hebrew text. Not praying, certainly not, just engaging in an available intellectual exercise, I managed to keep up to speed only with long familiar words and passages, stumbling haltingly through the rest. I toyed with the notion of taking a Hebrew class to increase my facility in the language, following the example of the man at my left who, having known no Hebrew when he became president of the congregation, had begun diligent study. Now he was doing well enough to lead the congregation in prayer. Still, it was comforting to note that his Hebrew was not much better than mine.

After one of the traditional prayers, the rabbi asked us to focus on ourselves for a few moments of silent meditation. We stood, covering our closed eyes with our hands, so that we could see within ourselves, she said. She gives new meaning to the concept of sanctuary, I thought. She wants this place, which does not even belong to us, to be a safe place for each of us. Safe from the world. Safe, even, from ourselves. *Kadosh, kadosh, kadosh.* Holy, holy, holy, felt the space in which I stood. Why had I even thought of not coming? Why don't I remember from week to week that this good space exists for me? No matter that the others are almost without exception much younger than I, that none of them are my friends, in the conventional sense. There was something here worth having.

I looked around and saw that others were already reseated. I settled back into my chair pensively. The rabbi was on my right. I watched her as she led us somberly through the Reader's Kaddish. Her eyes are sad and mournful. She understands death and loss and loneliness but she can tap into deep reservoirs of hopefulness. It is a miracle, I think, how filled with hope she is, despite everything, despite great sorrows of her own that she shares with us.

Then we were singing *Oseh Shalom Bim Ramov* and,

remembering and forgetting

unexpectedly, shockingly, I felt tears come to my eyes -- I don't do that sort of thing, I don't cry even when the situation calls for it -- but it was the same song, the same tune, that we used to sing around our Shabbat table on the Friday nights of that childhood life long ago that I never remember, and suddenly I was melting. The melody is the only residue of that life that habitually stirs good feelings for me and now I was weeping. I felt comforting hands come from both sides and meekly, gratefully, accepted the solace tendered me.

By the time my neighbor had taken out and unfolded a large white handkerchief to offer me, I was back in the world. I was not going to smear his generosity with my mascara. Are you all right? eyes asked me around the room. I was all right. But when it came to pass moments later that the rabbi started reading the Yahrzeit list, my father's name was one of those to be memorialized. How uncommonly apt that I chose to attend this morning, I thought, this morning of all mornings just as if I had planned to come to say Kaddish. Which is, it occurs to me, what everyone must think was on my mind when the tears began to flow. They would naturally presume that I was crying about my father's death but I wasn't because he never came to mind until this very moment although I am not gloating about that really I have no objection to weeping about my father even though I have not done it yet indeed it is high time that I do that it has been nine years since he died and I haven't wept a tear for him yet.

Are you all right? they asked afterwards. Of course, I am all right, I said. Thank you, I said, wishing I did not sound so stiff and stand-offish. The rabbi gave me a hug. Can I do something for you? she asked. You have, I said, and took her into my heart forever.

≈ ≈ ≈

remembering and forgetting

FUNTIME

I sit in the luxury of a penthouse apartment and look out at a vast expanse of rolling waters whose thunderous crashes against the shore are the morning's only sounds. A few hundred feet before my eyes an expertly choreographed company of sea gulls leaps and swoops, their wings alternately light and dark as they turn into and away from the rays of the rising sun. On cue, the birds having completed their presentation and flown gracefully from view, a sleek white toymaker's model of perfect shipness enters the scene smoothly from stage right and, obeying laws of optics that demand respect, transforms itself into a handsome ocean liner making its steadfast way across the sea.

"Do you want to go down to the beach or to play tennis first?" my travel companions ask me. I don't know what to say. I don't want anything, but I don't want to interfere with their pleasure either. Whatever they want to do is fine. Through the artfully arranged stems of silken flowers in the vase on my breakfast table, I watch the dark green sea pursue its morning exercise: small ripples and softly undulating waves move in random fashion until they are overtaken at regular intervals by the powerful forces moving them forward, forward and upward into their spectacular midair conversions into frothy white foam. The

remembering and forgetting

combination of force and purposefulness is awe-inspiring to behold but I am not so much awed as I am disappointed to realize once more (through a hasty glance at my perpetual emotional barometer) that the most breathtaking natural beauty leaves me wholly unaffected. My heart is hard; it refuses to sing with joy no matter how rationally I point out the wonders before me. As I have long known, I can be unhappy anywhere.

Vacation trips that brings dreams to life for the normal folk with whom I travel are wasted on me; they burden me with their subliminal imperatives to enjoy, enjoy. Although everything I see is wondrously beautiful, I cannot escape the knowledge that underneath the thin veneer of superficial beauty, the world's sadness is unabated. Although I will myself to enjoy all the proferred pleasures that extraordinary good luck has put in my path, I cannot put out of mind the misery in which most people are condemned to live out their lives. Life is not good for me if it is not good for all.

A tiny bird hops onto the tile floor of the balcony that overlooks the sea and lifts its head in cheerful song. "Be happy," it sings with a self-assurance so outrageous even I cannot help being amused, and flies off. Good advice, I think, put a smile on my face and join the others on the beach. It is the whitest, finest, most beautiful beach in the world, my friends assert with the conviction born out of careful analyses of many seashores; I think they may be right. The pure white sand that reaches out to the horizon feels warm and welcoming underfoot.

My friends are happy. The weatherman's prediction of showers was off the mark, and here we are, basking in the sunshine of another perfect day in paradise. What more can anyone want? The question, though uttered gaily, is meant for me. They cannot understand and so I do not say that there is nothing I want, nothing I can imagine, that would make me as happy as they seem to be. Nor do I want them to know the emptiness at the core of my being, the sadness that weighs me down, that spreads like an anti-life force from cell to cell. try to keep it from showing. I smile. I laugh. I sing and dance and engage in all the hedonistic activities that others find diverting. They have, after all, their own concerns. I do what I can to keep from making them unhappy too.

Once I had a soulmate who understood, who saw the world through the same off-colored lenses as I. She also, this darling aunt of blessed memory, she also had left Nazi Germany without visible wounds; she also had never been able to recover from her good fortune. She sought refuge in Palestine in the mid-thirties, committed herself to building a marriage and a nation and then gave up on both of them with what she thought at the time to be good reasons, in order to come to the United States.

"Are you happy?" she asked me one day as she helped me with the dishes of a Sunday night supper she had shared with us. I turned sharply and stared at her. The question was too direct, too unexpected. It gave me a jolt to think that my happiness, or lack of it, could be subject to anyone's speculation, even hers.

"Happy?" I said. "I don't know what that means. I have a good life, a wonderful family, everything I've ever wanted and more. So am I happy?"

"How would I know?" she answered, "I am still trying to figure it out. But this I know, that as long as one can keep a smile on one's face, one can maintain a facade of happiness. And that is important. Perhaps, where human happiness is concerned, facade is all there is."

Yes. That is just why I loved her. Because she shared my point of view -- my *Weltanschauung* -- so precisely and tried so valiantly to the end of her days to transcend it.

remembering and forgetting

More than anything, she wanted to avoid infecting others with her sadness. She too, given the opportunity, would have lain in the glorious Florida sunshine with an artificial smile on her face and wondered how, after Auschwitz, people manage to live normal happy lives.

I think of her as I agree, with no appetite for food whatsoever, to walk down the beach to share a few dozen fresh oysters.

Facade may not be all, but it is better than nothing; I cling tightly to mine.

≈≈≈

remembering and forgetting

LIKE A SICKNESS

I splashed a handful of cold water on my face. I had to get myself moving. I was already late in getting dressed for the evening's activity: a fundraiser for a human rights organization with which I had recently had a shorter professional association than I had hoped to have. I no longer had any bad feelings about being fired and thought I wanted to prove that by attending so I said OK when my friends touted the event but now that the time had come, I really did not want to go.

I am always having to dress for events I don't want to attend because I am generally so passive about such things that I rarely say, or know, what I want to do for an evening and regularly allow others to make my social plans for me. This time I could not blame the decision to attend on my husband because he was even less enthusiastic about going than I was. His reluctance was, moreover, a matter of principle. They had not been fair to me.

"Let's not go," I said with more energy than I felt, watching him watch me as I applied a thin layer of sheer makeup to my face. "You can see the ballgame and I can read. We'll both be happier. Besides, they already have

remembering and forgetting

our money. As long as we have no desire to go and no shred of obligation at this point, doesn't it make more sense to just stay home?"

In the mirror, I saw him smiling as he adjusted his tie. "Sure. Sure. We will stay home and they will think that even after a year you don't have the courage to face them. I wouldn't give the bastards that satisfaction. Or, and this is even more likely, they won't think that at all but by tomorrow morning you will have persuaded your-self that they do and will hate yourself for not going. Much as I want to stay in, I think I would rather suffer through a dull party tonight than through all those recriminations tomorrow."

He knows me too well. I tried to argue that I had no reservations about the party other than the certainty of incredible boredom but eventually I yielded to his good sense. We went, and soon found ourselves at a generic middle class fundraising event, a glance around the room serving quickly to confirm the presence of the usual *hors d'oeuvres*, the usual beverages, and the usual people standing around in small clusters of conversation.

For a moment I wondered again why we had come and then I recognized Joe, a white-haired gentleman I had been accustomed to seeing regularly while he was volunteering and I was a staff person for the organization. Our weekly encounters had been part of a socially useful and diverting retirement activity for him while I was investing my energies into another of a series of low-pay, high-moral-vision jobs through which I keep trying to make the world better.

Having caught my eye, Joe broke away from the small group he was regaling with World War II anecdotes and walked across the small distance between us with a great flourish, holding his arms wide open while greeting me effusively. Evidently, the wine had been flowing. He put his hands on my shoulders as if we were old friends instead of fond acquaintances and tilted his head back to take a good look at me.

"It is wonderful to see you here. You know, it is not the same without you at the old place," he said. "Wednesdays aren't much fun anymore, with you gone."

I found this dramatic if minor expression of support incredibly moving, and responded in kind. "I know. At first, I missed it too," I said slowly, sensing that I was packing my words densely with meaning. "For a while, it was like a sickness. But I got over it."

I was smiling as I said it but the statement re-sounded in my head. Joe began telling a story about a complaint that he had recently handled but I could not follow the point he was making although I did manage to make sounds appropriate to comprehension and affirmation while inwardly replaying my own words with a rush of pride at having painted my separation experience so metaphorically. How clever I was to make the subtle analogy between missing that job and a sickness, I thought for a brief instant, until the realization exploded in my head that there was nothing at all metaphoric about the dialogue and I felt beads of cold sweat at the back of my neck.

Like a sickness? That was putting it mildly. The end of that job had plunged me straight back into the sickness that does not end. One day I was working and the next day I was not. The abrupt ending was morally and rationally defensible but emotionally it was devastating. Intending to have no regrets, reasoning coolly that I was better off rid of the yoke under which I had been working in tandem with an obsessively paranoid partner, I no sooner had unstructured, purposeless days to fill once more than I saw disaster coming. In no time I was standing on the track with the express train speeding toward me. What to dooooooooooo? what to doooooooooooooooooo? it howled as it aimed for me. There was no getting out of its way. I was paralyzed

remembering and forgetting

before it and in no time it knocked me low, low, low, until I was trembling at the edge of the abyss with nowhere to go but down, once again as purposeless and aimless as the day my little one left for kindergarten.

In that abyss into which I fall, there are no tears, there is no sadness. There are no recriminations. There is no hope, no appetite for food or life, no pleasurable moment, no capacity for planning, no speck of inner peace. There is no justification for my existence, no reason for living, no hope for tomorrow and no end to today. There is nothing but nothingness without end.

And then one day I see the light again and it is over. For the moment, at least, it is over. For despair is like a sickness, like a chronic sickness. One gets better, and one gets worse, but one doesn't get over it. Despite what one says when the occasion demands it to casual acquaintances, one definitely does not get over it. Once one has become aware of the bottom of the abyss, the awareness is omnipresent and every minor fall from grace becomes a reminder that our small efforts can make little ultimate impact against the immutable human capacity for evil, against the impossibility of perfecting the world.

How hard it must be to be God facing this flawed universe, I can only imagine. How hard it is not to be God, I have long known.

"Joe, my friend, what was it you were saying? My mind wandered for a moment. It's such fun getting together with like-minded people, isn't it? and trying to make a difference?"

≈≈≈

remembering and forgetting

OBJECTIVE ANALYSIS

I look at this child and think for a moment how wonderful she is and immediately I stop myself. She is darling, yes, and precious too, but highly unusual? Probably not. It astonishes me to find myself thinking her exceptional, when I have always been burdened with such an excess of objectivity that I could never understand, even as a child, how others could, unquestioningly, call their mothers or fathers or even their favorite books or toys, the best in the world. Mine were good, and perhaps better than some, I had always reasoned, but to establish primacy one would have to have more facts than I, or the others, could possibly have available.

Making personal assessments as a function of mind rather than heart was a fact of life that I did not choose, would not have chosen, but which I recognized at a precocious age, and which early convinced me that I was congenitally incapable of truly loving anyone. Even at my own children -- much later -- I could look only with cold, objective eyes. So of course it is a wonderment that this little person who is clearly no more gorgeous nor more brilliant than other children affects me so strongly. She is so amusing to me, such a pleasure to observe, such a delight to hold in my arms, I can scarcely believe myself. I

remembering and forgetting

never seem to tire of her presence.

This little one is eighteen months old and walks and talks and has temper tantrums very much like other eighteen-month old children. A month or so ago, I would have described her as just another wonderful child but in the last few weeks, when she has been with me a little more than usual while I cared for her during a brief illness that would otherwise have caused chaos in the work schedule of her mother, my daughter, I have found myself rethinking my assessment.

It seemed at first natural enough, she being such an adorable child, for me to adore her until it struck me how unnatural, in fact, that is for me, the perception of pleasure being in itself a rare experience for me. And not only was I becoming attached to her but she to me as well. That became clear one recent evening at a family celebration at which she, the only toddler in attendance, took center stage by willfully drawing me and then adults she barely knew into joining her in playing "Ring Around the Rosie".

Six-foot tall men and elegantly dressed women were surprised to find themselves sprawled on the floor to the tune of Ashes, Ashes, All Fall Down, shortly after submitting to the irresistible beckoning of her tiny but commanding hand. She had used her winning ways for hours before her amiability began slowly to fade.

By then, we had gathered together under the stars in a circle for a havdala service, thirty or forty people linked together in unconscious imitation of an ancient tribal rite, faces shimmering in moon- and candlelight. An almost mystical stillness was shattered in the instant that the now very tired baby, in her mother's arms the space of a few people away from me, cried and reached out for me. Generously, graciously, my daughter yielded the love of her life over to me, and, as the small arms circled my neck and the little head dropped onto my chest, I heard the young

remembering and forgetting

woman standing next to us say, with a note of awed astonishment in her voice, my goodness, she really loves you.

Yes. Yes. She really does. It is always a surprise to me too that someone should love me. I snuggled the child against my body until the service ended, and then, reluctantly, returned her to her mother's arms. I felt not deprived but strangely serene, a feeling I tried to recapture a few hours later when I awoke from a brief sleep and knew that my night's rest had ended. My mind was in a jumble. In no mood for the mental processing that often keeps my brain churning, I tried deep breathing, then moved to another room to read an obscure analysis of the golem in Jewish thought.

It did not work. After an hour of such futile attempts to slow down the activity in my head, only my eyes were tired. I turned off the light, closed my eyes and gave in to the questions waiting for my attention: what is it that keeps me awake and impossibly restless when I have had a perfect evening, enjoying the company of family members that I love? what more do I want? why don't I sleep like a baby after such a pleasant experience?

This has to be under my control, I thought. I am doing this to myself, I know. But why, why? Is there perhaps a part of me that likes the agitation from which I suffer, likes it for perverse reasons I do not understand? can it be that I actually make myself miserable because somehow, at the deepest levels of my being, I do not believe I deserve to feel good, that I punish myself for being so lucky as to be saved? Yes, that is part of it, of course. Objectively, there can be no explanation for my fortuitous escape from a cruel destiny. It is certainly not deserved. In a just universe, there would be no chance for an imperfect person like myself to be spared the cruelties that befell the slaughtered innocents of the Holocaust, cruelties that no one, ever, deserved. Certain that I deserve suffering as much, or as little, as anyone, could it be that I aim, not objectively but unconsciously, to make the universe more just by assuming suffering not merited by my actual experience?

As I am proceeding coolly, rationally, with this unplanned self-analysis, I see myself suddenly a child again, remembering myself alone and feverish in a sickbed in a strange new country while my parents are at work and the glaring lights over my head are spinning toward me and my bed is swaying and the walls are caving in and I want somebody to take care of me and there is no one but me to do the caring.

I jump up to quell the anxiety that is about to burst into full flame again and, in a flash of insight, I recognize the needy, needy child that is still with me, the one whose cries and yammerings I have tried so hard not to hear. Perhaps -- despite my long-standing resistance to the notion -- there has been a secondary gain connected to my recent weeks, months, of mental anguish and from my life-long history of psychosomatic ailments: I make myself sick enough so that, at last, someone will notice me and love me and take care of me and provide the safe world I have always yearned for.

And it occurs to me what the attachment to this precious child is, that somehow I am using her to nurture my inner child, giving her all the unconditional love that I wanted, needed, as a young child; it was no accident that my mother described me as being *"Liebesbedürftig"*, using the all but untranslatable and only slightly pejorative German expression connoting a neediness for love. And she, this adorable creature, in accepting and reciprocating in full measure, is healing me, filling me with love.

Even I find it hard to be objective about that.

remembering and forgetting

SUITE 1000

The room is small but stark and unrelenting. Hard chairs, hard walls, unbroken by the smallest opening for normal communication with anyone within the inner chambers, create an oppressive atmosphere not lightened one iota by the five small buzzers aligned vertically along the edge of an inner door to serve in lieu of receptionist for the professionals listed on the interspersed name plates. The name plates are themselves so discreet as to be almost unnoticeable, as if meant to deflect attention. It is a small victory to select the right one. A tentative pressure on the chosen button yields only silence. After that, nothing.

What can you do? Once you see that there is no one to greet, no one with whom to check the time of an appointment, no one to provide assurance that the doctor is in, you sit down and wait as if it is the most normal thing in the world to walk into a room, ring a doorbell and be ignored. And then you stew. Have you rung the right bell? Have you come on the right day? At the right time? To the right place?

There's no point in looking to others. Usually there is no one in the room. If anyone else is present, as occasionally there is, it is worse than being alone. Inevitably the

remembering and forgetting

other person melts into the walls as if in obedience to an unwritten but easily perceived dictum that social interchange is not welcome in this space. Inside their own invisible cocoons, the waiting folk concentrate their psychic energies on the defense of their individual anonymities, by steadfast reading and polite restraint from acknowledging any new arrival until, one by one, each person is summoned within by the various professionals with their identically bland and equally generic, unsmiling, peremptory, invitations to "come in".

I am getting used to this weird setting but I don't much like it. The clear fact that the psychological ambience is as carefully designed as the physical setting makes me wonder what esoteric rules are at the heart of the quasitherapeutic game in which I am enmeshed. I am not sure why I bring myself to this miserable place. I am neither a talented player of games nor a malleable pawn in the games of others.

And yet. Life is a game, isn't it? And I am losing. I play by my own rules and they are wrong. I know that but what can I do? Not only can I not play by rules that make no sense to me, I have no real interest in winning or even in playing. I sit on the sidelines and watch others contending for goals that are meaningless to me. What motivates them to struggle for such empty victories? What does it matter who wins, who loses? Could I run as fast, kick as hard and true? I don't know and I won't try to find out. I simply don't play.

I have taken myself out of the running. It is my choice, not someone else's (though I remember, long ago, how awful it was not to be selected in those playground games for which I was never dexterous, agile, quick, popular enough) because I do not like games in which some are chosen and others rejected. I have no interest in being included so that someone else may be excluded. I am too aware of the pain such choices involve (always in the background, in the not-to-be-suppressed underside of consciousness: the memorable, horrendous choices of this century, made in the death camps where bureaucrats determined who should live and who should die with silent wrist movements).

If choosing and rejecting, or being chosen or rejected, are difficult aspects of game playing, winning and losing are even more troublesome. I simply see no pleasure to be found in games that some must lose so others can win. It is a constant source of wonderment that people can rejoice in winning and totally disregard the pain of the losers. I never lose sight of the fact that every victory won is a defeat for someone else. I am not talking about war games here. I am talking about base-ball, tennis, card games, politics. Were you to suggest that this is an exaggerated and unfounded sensibility, I would not argue.

I am hypersensitive to pain as well and not in myself alone. I feel the pain of others, sometimes more than they do. The mere sight of someone in pain can make me nauseous. Show me a bloody wound, a broken limb, a videotaped surgical operation, and I feel real, authentic, no-kidding-about-it physical pain at the base of my spinal column where I have a vestigial pain receptor otherwise unknown in the species to which I belong. Give me the news of the latest devastation by cyclone in Bangladesh or revolution in South America and the pain shoots up my spine.

Is that pain psychological? No, no more than any pain caused by any wound is psychological. The pain is real and in the flesh, even if it rises out of the nebulous regions of the mind-body interface. What good is it, this excessive, atypical, sensitivity to pain? None. None, whatsoever. I see it as a weakness, a step backward on the evolutionary continuum and no help to anyone, especially not to me.

remembering and forgetting

Because I am weary of all the redundancy, I take myself to this place to redefine myself, to get rid of the pain, once and for all. I am so tired of the tiredness, so sick of the sickness, so bored with the boredom. I want to redo myself, make myself over, according to a standard model, become like others. Here they think that talking about it will help, that I will come to see that I am as good as anybody. If I will just see the sense of their rules.

Right. Deal me in.

≈≈≈

remembering and forgetting

DREAMING

A jagged scratch on the wooden chair leg caught my eye and had me hypothesizing about its likely causes until the crushed and utterly demoralized loops in the twisted yarn of the carpet demanded my immediate and critical attention. Concentrate, concentrate, I urged myself, wishing I could stop being distracted from the business at hand. I was trying to look inward, searching for something meaningful to recount and could find nothing, nothing worth noting.

Nothing, nothing at all, worthy or unworthy of note. The intrinsic futility of the task was not lost on me. Rationally considered, it is not possible to look inward, and if it were possible, it occurred to me that I would not want to see a maze of blood vessels and twisted nerve endings. With annoyance, I mentally pushed aside the fleeting intrusion of a partially recalled glossy illustration of opthalmic connections and redirected my energies to finding something in my head worth saying.

I was studying the pattern behind the carpet loops again when he broke the silence.

"So what did you dream last night?"

remembering and forgetting

I tried not to laugh. It was hard not to feel sorry for the man. He was asking that question again, innocently again, as if for the first time, as if he expected me to answer. The smallest dream fragments would, I knew from experience, elicit the highest praise from him but I was once more unable to deliver even the hint of a dream. The truth, which he simply refuses to accept, is that I never dream. I see him smile as I think this. "Everybody dreams," he says. "You withhold."

Truly, I never dream, at least not in the sense other people dream, creating fantastic narratives in which they star as victims or heroes or even spectators, in their own or symbolic guises. Naturally, I would like to dream like that, would like nothing better than to demonstrate by the enthralling intricacy of my dreams the so-far unnoticed creativity of my unconscious mind. If dreams are the key to my cure, and he certainly thinks so, I want to dream multitudes of them, remember them, deliver them, analyze them. I want to please him and, more, to cooperate in the unraveling of the unconscious processes that keep me bound.

Why would I choose to stand in my own way by hiding my dreams, or worse, by not dreaming? We quarrel about this now and again. He thinks I could dream, do dream, but don't want, for some perverse reason not clear to me, to know about it. I try to explain that I do not have the requisite imagination, that my unconscious mind is dull and plodding and not given to visual expression.

The artistic cells are missing or, at the very least, are in total submission to the clerical cells, which convert all the subconscious processes triggered by sleep into redundant mechanical operations on whose behalf my psychic motor huffs and puffs diligently all night long so that I regularly awaken exhausted from what seem to be hours of endless and inexplicable filing or alphabetizing or sorting of God only knows what. Night after night, I work at the same meaningless repetitive tasks while I sleep. Night after night, I fall asleep willing myself to dream and disobey myself by filing, filing, filing.

"Dream?", I asked in response, trying not to sound condescending. "I dreamed nothing. You know that. You know I do not dream. I am a practical person. I do not deal in symbols. I am direct. If I am depressed, I need not conjure up a dream well to symbolize the depths to which I have fallen. The abyss is all around me when I am awake. When conscious images do the job for me, why should I need to dream?"

"Everybody dreams," he said.

Except me, I said, and meant it.

And then, this. I went to sleep one night and found myself nearing a bloody mangled object that one glance told me was a dead animal lying in the road on which I was traveling. In the same instant I knew that it was not real, that I was dreaming, but even so I could not look at it and so quickly averted my eyes and kept moving but just for a brief moment before I stopped myself, thinking to myself, dreaming all the while, thinking, wait a minute, wait just a minute here, you can't just walk by, can't just turn away, maybe what you see is not a dead animal, maybe it is a living animal or even a human being in pain that can be helped and so I turned and looked until I could readily discern the shape and could see that the object in the road was, yes, was actually the back side of a seated person, now appearing not so much mangled as wholly bloody and unskinned. In my sleep I shuddered. It was not a view I could tolerate, waking or sleeping, even though I had no sense that it was anyone I know or ever knew and I put a quick end to the whole experience by waking myself and running quickly through the powers of two to end my agitation.

remembering and forgetting

    For months I managed to put the bloody dream object out of mind and then one day the sight of a mangled creature on the highway caused me to avert my eyes and to recall, instantaneously, the hideous dream image to consciousness.

    And, just as suddenly, it was clear. Of course, I withhold, even from myself. He was right. I run away from my own dreams, afraid to see them out, just as I look selectively at what real life has to show me. Yes, despite all my claims to objectivity and rationality, I look out at the world through narrow slits of eyes trying to see only the good and the beautiful, trying to protect myself from the ugly and the painful.

    Even in movie theaters, I shield my fragile psyche from the sight of simulated pain, from bloody ketchupped wounds and imitation fights and from any other cinematic views that might further unsettle my already unsettled world view. In the darkness in which I cower, I often observe myself, objectively, to be the only one watching a fictional massacre with my hands over my eyes, the only one to feel that there is no such thing as a fictional massacre since every imaginable violence and every conceivable cruelty has already been committed an infinite number of times in reality.

    It is a harshly alienating experience, this repeated recognition that my appetite for violence is so abnormally low that I cannot tolerate violence in the same spirit of fun that others do. Without ever having experienced any, I have had my fill of violence. The Shoah, it seems, provided all I'll ever need along those lines. I need no more, want no more, can stand no more, even of indirect experience. I am constantly amazed that others who must have witnessed the same events I have observed have not yet had their fill of gratuitous violence; they seem somehow able to keep integrating the knowledge of more and more refinements of violence and cruelty into their understanding of human nature without feeling a trace of existential disgust.

Perhaps, then, I was wrong in saying I do not dream. Perhaps I do dream but kill my dreams quickly and efficiently with whatever unconscious and subconscious forces I can summon while sleeping and then busy myself, night after night, with filing, filing, filing, so that I will be too busy to dream on. Perhaps all the redundant processes that keep me so busy in my sleep are designed to protect me from dreaming the dream I am most afraid of dreaming, the one in which I will see my grandmother bent over the edge of a large hole in the earth and she is wearing nothing but a rag and she is digging, digging. Can I help you, Oma? I ask. I want to help her, she was so good to me and, what is more, I owe her. She saved my life when I was little and choking by holding me tight and pounding my back until the foreign object in my throat was dislodged. Yes, she says, kill me, kill me if you love me, and I see her lying in the hole, bloodied and raw, writhing like the carp we once brought home not yet altogether dead. Kill me, kill me, she says, and I can't do it though I want very much to do it, know that she wants me to do it, but I can't lift a finger. I can't get my dress dirty, it is time for school, I am not sup-posed to be late, and I run off but I don't know which way to go and I am lost and I cannot stop running.

I haven't dreamed it yet. If I am careful, perhaps I never will.

≈ ≈ ≈

remembering and forgetting

NOT YET

It is strange, I know, for me to be so Holocaust-obsessed when I am not even a "survivor" and, God knows, I am not a survivor. Just because I was there and am here, because I got out of the wrong place at the right time, so to say, does not make me a survivor. I reserve that term, with deference, for those who suffered directly from the genocidal solution of the Nazis to their perceived Jewish problem: those who suffered untold and untellable horrors in the extermination camps, those who saw their loved ones torn from their grasp and brutalized before their eyes, those who starved, crawled, scrambled, fought and bled their way through the fire of Hell to eventual safety and freedom.

I experienced no such trauma. Lucky as I was, I came away with my life, and my mother and father as well, landing safely in America without ever having been physically violated and without ever having seen a concentration camp. I have no scar, no tattooed number on my arm, to give evidence of my presence on the scene of the Crime. Why then is my head so full of Holocaust, so full that it is hardly good for anything but carting around the sadness? Why cannot I forget, like others have, that ten million fellow human beings were done away with in one absurd cosmic joke at which one would have to be insane to laugh?

Perhaps, without ever knowing Eden, I have eaten the forbidden fruit, and am forced to endure the inescapable punishment. Expelled from innocence, I must live out my days with the overwhelming knowledge of infinite evil. That knowledge blocks everything else from my mind, including the desire to know more about the Holocaust. On the contrary, I no longer search for answers to my questions. I need no more facts or theories, explanations or excuses. I resign myself to never understanding how it is possible that the Holocaust occurred, nor how it is possible for some people to deny that it occurred. Nor will I ever understand the seemingly natural ability of human beings to inflict great cruelties on one another, even on a small scale. I don't expect to ever understand cruelty at all.

I would be content to understand myself, and why I cannot, through a sheer act of will, shift my psyche into a more optimistic gear, even though nothing terrible happened to me. .Nothing.

I don't know why I can't let go.

I don't know why I can't put an end to my sorrow when I know full well how fortunate I am, that I am on the receiving end of more love than most people ever experience. I don't know why my most zealous efforts to channel my energies into constructive endeavors outside of myself cannot produce anything that seems useful to me, cannot block from consciousness the personal and global hopelessness with which I was so early infected, cannot end the periodic lapses into inertia and despair.

I don't know why I cannot make a saving leap of faith to God when it is clear to me that faith in a super-natural and omnipotent power is the most rational justification for

remembering and forgetting

optimism, or why I cannot at least promulgate, for altruistic reasons, the kind of cheerful world view in which my beloved rabbi claims to believe when she declares that the Messiah will come to perfect the now broken world when all of us are performing good deeds at the same time.

Someday, perhaps, I will be able to claim such a saving belief for myself. Someday, when the taste of cyanide is no longer in my mouth, when the smell of fire no longer comes to my nostrils in the midst of a perfect spring garden, I will be like other people, and get on with living.

Some day. Not yet. Not yet.

≈≈≈

remembering and forgetting

AFTERWORD

Eighteen years have flown over and through me since I committed these depressed and depressive ruminations to writing, and much has changed that might be worth noting but only one thing needs to be said, and it contradicts everything that precedes it: I am happy. Despite my long-held conviction that I would never reach a state of grace in which I could honestly report such a thing, I am happy. Despite everything I know to be true about the world, I have managed to manipulate my brain into accepting happiness as its primary frame of reference, the backdrop against which everything else falls. I have dropped as excess baggage my obsession with the Holocaust, though I have not stopped grieving its effects or its unfortunate reflection of the extent of human imperfection.

Take yesterday. It was my birthday, my seventy-seventh, and a perfectly glorious day. Not a moment of its crystalline beauty escaped my notice. My husband brought me presents in bed and showered me with personal and electronic wishes of a curiously sentimental and touching kind. Over coffee I observed a slew of handsome young men cavorting around in the upper branches of our trees, cutting out deadwood, in an athletic display of artistry silhouetted against a perfect blue sky that was surely a

remembering and forgetting

special gift to mark the day.

 Birthday wishes came piling in. I received calls and greetings from loving souls around the world, friends in Israel and Mexico, children in their widespread locations, and grandchildren, also widely distributed, as well as dear friends nearby. Each call, each email message, seemed like a gift of immeasurable value. I felt, over and over again, the infinite power of infinite love. I had a simple lunch with a friend. It was all pleasure. I had a perfect dinner with all my closest family members who live in town, and I enjoyed every morsel, every moment.

 I don't have a word for my current state of mind, which harbors no bitterness, no rancor, no regrets. I cannot explain it. The world continues to be fraught with dangers. My mother teeters at the edge of death, and I myself am not getting younger, but life has never seemed more beautiful, more filled with possibilities. And every cell in my body overflows with gratitude for my good fortune.

 It is a surprise ending for this story, I suppose. And no one is more surprised by it than I.

≈≈ 12/20/07 ≈≈

remembering and forgetting

poems

Resuffering

Resuffering the past,
presuffering the future,
allows me no rest.
Night after night I close my eyes
and somehow see it all again:
myself high on Moriah again,
On top of that wood again,
knife at my throat again,
ready to breathe my last again,

And I tremble again,
exceedingly tremble again,
and I am saved again.
Why am I saved again?
Save the others, I say,
Save the six million, I say,
And he says No again,
and I must wake again
and wonder why.

≈≈9/1/91 ≈≈

PSALM 1987

Enough! saith the Lord.

I have heard more lamentations
and pious exhortations than I can bear,
for all your public grief perplexes me.
How arrogantly you rave on about the Horror
while I, your God, stay silent
in the agony of unspeakableness,
pondering yet the dumbstriking mystery,
the holy burning mystery of the slaughter
of six million of my children.
How is it you dare brazenly to touch
the still white-burning flame and
fear not to be consumed?

Remember! saith the Lord.

Since first I showed you good and evil
and commanded you to walk in righteous paths,
I have seen you strive toward goodness
for my Name's sake.
And since first you learned the
quintessential moral choice,
you have, in many times and places
and against great odds,
remembered to choose life,
and to enhance it, in my Name.
Why now then do you build
monuments to death and suffering,
meant to enhance not my Name but yours?

What perverse pride moves you,
for common pity's sake, to prattle on about
the uncommon anguish of your people?
No good will come of all these mournful lessons,
no good at all. Or do you think parading
griefs before the world
will stave off further grief?
that airing old deep wounds
will heal humanity's ills?

or, least probable of all, that
broadcasting my powerlessness
will make the world --
and your own children --
love, honor and revere me?

Listen! saith the Lord.

The world is what it is;
it will not be a better place
because past evils are repackaged
and displayed anew
to those whose hearts are innocent
of the awful truths that torment me,
and some of you. End your charades.
I want no more graven images,
no more stone memorials,
no more public tears from weepers
in designer clothes
whose guilt-edged sorrow dissolves
at program's end.

Give me, please, no more recriminations
against those who might have done
more or less or somehow otherwise
nor one more rosy bright morality tale
which paints silver linings on the clouds
of smoke over the crematoria.

What was, was, saith the Lord.

Only one commemoration serves my will:
to remember in silence -- in sorrow and ashes --
all the evils that humans commit against each other
and then to rise again, to choose life again,
to hope again, and to strive for righteousness
again because it is my will, and yours.

≈≈4/27/87≈≈

Letter from Home, November 1941

Dearest ones, it is bitter cold in Germany.
My old bones shudder as I write, but you --
I hear from Cousin Ida -- are doing fine,
resettled now in the warm lap of Amerika.
You know I never was so much a family man
and I can manage if I have to on my own,
though I am far from liking it one little bit.
You are warm, are you? In Germany it's cold.

No mail gets through, and no one cooks for me.
Your mother has the last laugh on me now,
she who felt the stinging cold before it came,
she strangely now the fortunate one,
having died of a different, more natural chill.
Lucky she, warmer in her grave than I above.
I ask for nothing, dear ones. I have no right.
Was I not always -- ach, I could regret it now
if regrets made sense -- but yes too busy
to attend to my good wife, or you, my dears?
The good just God in Heaven knows what
He does, dear ones, so it is right and fitting
that you are in Amerika and I here in the cold.
I am old enough to die. Still, I'm young enough
to live -- you understand?

If you should get this letter, take it as a sign
that God is kind and will not mind your starting
up the paperwork for me, speedily, while papers
still can help. Can you do that for me,
dear ones? if you have the time?

I want only to be warm once more before I die.

≈≈6/17/91≈≈

Written in memory of Adolf Spiegel, my grandfather

Around the World in 80 Years

In Münster he made five-cornered hats for bishops.
Don't laugh. It was no joke, it was a business,
a way to make a decent living, sort of,
in a time when just living was for a Jew
a funny business. He wasn't very Jewish,
He felt German. At that you could laugh.
Since God was altogether dead, he said,
it made no sense at all to cling for life
to an obsolete and quite ungermanic faith.
He married a Gentile woman to prove the point.

In Dachau he wore stripes and spat at guards
who saw such unions as crimes against the race.
He planned escapes, wild fuzzy and impractical plans
with no chance at all to work until one did.
The goosestepping louts who called the shots
and shot them too hit him four times as he ran out,
and yet he got away. To China. Who could believe it?
In Shanghai he nursed his wounds and starved.
The Red Cross sent an SOS. Your brother's dying
Stop. Has no money for daily bowl of rice.
Stop. Send help. Stop. We found some dollars
here and there to help. He came to America
a broken man and never had a thing to say.
And we, we never had a thing to ask him.

In New York he drew and worked out puzzles.
For fifty years he moved the jagged pieces
to and fro to make them fit but in the puzzle
of his life one gaping hole would not be filled:
the space left by the beautiful gentile Maria,
when, long ago, a precision bomb made in the USA
exploded in their Münster home one fine spring day.
To the end he kept his silence as he drew lush green
Edens overgrown with tiny black five-cornered hats.

≈≈6/1991≈≈

Written in memory of, my uncle. Ludwig Spiegel

American Girl

In the long black dress I wore
that night, I was beautiful, they said,
and David Gordon wrote a poem
not the least bit lyrical about
roses being red and violets blue
which, though short of including
an iota of romantic sentiment
nonetheless enhanced the grace
of the fragrant buds he brought
and pinned deftly to my shoulder strap
to crown his mitzvah, his good deed,
for the day, the week, the year,
for which I am still grateful
even now, a lifetime later,
such an outright gift it was that
this handsome rabbi's son should
choose to take me to the prom,
me, the refugee girl from somewhere
that the boys routinely called
for homework help, not dates.

I was young, sixteen and altogether
naive in the the ways of the world
I lived in, believing I'd win male hearts
with math answers and generous
aid with their science stuff.
But in the rose-adorned black slinkiness
of that night, I became, briefly, briefly,
so typically the American Girl
that I wished with all my heart I was
but definitely wasn't, never forgetting
that I was lucky to be alive, not burned
into smoke in some crematorium
back home where I came from,
way on the other side
of the railroad tracks.

≈≈3/05/03 ≈≈

Beads of Perfection

Dawdling, looking at nothing, fiddling
mindlessly with the God-and-life-puzzle
that keeps gaining in complexity,
my eyes catch through the window
a dazzling sight that takes my breath:
bright glistening strings of minuscule
yet exquisite beads of water
leaping in perfect parallel arcs
into and through the verdant lushness,
each bead a globe as iridescent
as a perfect pearl,
reflecting the bluest blue of sky within
the radiant luster of infinity.

My heart skips a beat before I see
it's the automated sprinkler system --
not any kind of miracle at work,
but as I watch the programmed pattern
retrace its visible perfections,
gloriously redundant, merrily alive,
I sense for a moment I've found God,
waiting to be found, in this corner
of the garden seen from the window
I pass hourly; here in this instant:
perfect beauty, perfect harmony,
waiting, yes, and found.
The rainbow that now arches softly
over the dancing waters adds nothing,
can add nothing. The space
is filled with godliness.
And so, I find, am I.

≈≈ *6/6/99* ≈≈

In the Beginning

In the beginning
when time was born
and space burst into being
with planets, galaxies
and stars, whirling, turning
spinning, and the sun crashed
its way into the heavens,
there was amazing beauty

but no one was amazed at all;
there was no one to care,
no one to see, to praise,
the beauty or the symmetry, so --
without amazement -- or any
bemoaning the lack of amazement--
the universal dance went on,
without much notice

No question it was good --
just no one to say it was good --
until we came along. And saw.
And were amazed.
We knew that it was good
and said so. It is perhaps
our saying so,
our endless saying so,
that makes the universe
complete.

≈≈ 3/07/01 ≈≈

Giving Life to the Dead

    I.   *Gevurot/Strength*

When long ago the rabbis said,
you, God, are the hero of all,
you give life to the dead,
perhaps they meant to say --
at least some of them --
just this: great is our god,
who gives life to the unborn,
who makes the difference, and
who is the difference between
flesh and stone, between the
living and the not-living,
and that is power unlike
any other that humans see,

and when they said, Adonai
you are great to save,
they must have meant this too
that the thin small breath that
separates life from death
and death from life is god
and that holy holy holy
is the mystery of life.....

    II.   *Gevurot*/Resurrection

Life being short
it's small wonder
they thought, dreamed, imagined,
hoped, prayed, and finally believed
that death was not the end,
that God, the source of life,
not only could but would
with certainty one day
reverse the harsh finality
of death and bring back
when all was said and done
the loved ones that
had died too soon, all the dead

in fact, the loved and the unloved,
from generations past and future
back to some earthly Eden where,
when the Messiah comes,
we all might revel in the harmony
of peace and love and perfect comfort
leaving behind our then-and-now
discomfitures, disappointments
and regrets.
Who could nay-say such hopes, such
longed for opiates for bitter lives?
who could forswear the possibility
that someday at the end of time the
eagerly longed for would chance to be?
No one. Even the brilliant Maimonides,
physician to the court of Spain and
knowledgeable in matters of life and
death regarded it a necessary principle,
a requisite of Jewish faith, that
the dead will rise when the Messiah comes.

They believe it so, he thought,
perhaps it's true. But he knew better,
for, surely, when the Messiah comes,
we will all give up our greedy yearnings,
and let our loved ones
rest in holy peace, and we
ourselves will be at peace.

≈≈ *6/23/01* ≈≈

July Mourning

It's July again, and so soon
again it's his Yahrzeit,
that somber anniversary
we use to ritually remember,
to re-feel the grieving,
the loving and the living,
and to connect deeply
with the everlasting presence
in our hearts and souls
of a loved one lost to death

And we stand like
perpetual mourners of Zion.
Together and apart
we stand and remember
each our own grievous loss,
I saying kaddish for my dad
(victim now twenty years past
to a momentary slip,
an instant's loss of focus,
on the part of a good and
highly practiced surgeon)
while around me stand others
who've been bereaved
of a mother or father or sibling,
equally beloved, and even some
who've had an adored child
torn untimely
from their futile grasp.

We stand like mourners of Zion
reminded once again that
death and loss are part of life,
all life, and not just our own.
Together and apart we mourn --
of course we mourn! --

for we can sense the briefness
of our turn as mourner
in the cycle turning, turning,
to the day it is our own death
that's mourned

So we stand with all
the mourners of Zion,
and say, as our fathers
and mothers before us said,
and rightly,
blessed is the source of life
and blessed too
the chance we have
to live and breathe and love
and hope for peace.

≈≈ 7/15/01 ≈≈

Written in memory of my father, Julius Spiegel

Mother's Day

I.
"Do you remember that day?
what you did that day?
what you thought?"
she asked me out of the blue
and yet I knew
what day she meant.

"I had an abortion once,"
she said as if I hadn't heard,
"and I came back from Münster
on the train and meant to
take a taxi home but instead
walking ever so slow with a
big towel between my legs
to stanch the bleeding
I took tiny steps all the way
home from the station."

"You and Daddy were in
the kitchen, eating supper,"
she said, "when I finally
came home, still bleeding.
I wonder what you thought
when you saw me come in
like that." Me too.
I wonder what thought,
then so naive I still
believed storks brought babies
and the world was
a safe place in which to live.

II.
"I think I have been so
lucky," she says, again.
"I've had a good life,

a wonderful husband, and
children I am proud of.
And I've always had men
in love with me. Always.
Even my brother-in-law
who had a wife of his own
was always after me,
always trying to get
close to me, one time
going so far as to board
a train I was taking to
Berlin, so he could be
with me just until the
next stop. There I threw
him off. And there was
Alfred who hung around
for years just to hang
around, so much that
his mother came to me
and asked me to let go
of him so he could marry
and I said I'm not holding
him, he can go if he wants.
And also Walter who said he
would give up ten years
of his life if he could
just have me in his arms
for one night.

"I always said no. There
was only one man for me.
And do you know what he
said to me when he
left for the hospital for
the last time? he said, I
love you as much now as I
did the day we were married.
He really loved me. So
I know I am lucky. Yes.
There are men even now
who think they love me."
It is the measure of her life.

III.

"You know, I had an abortion
once, but I have no regrets.
It was no time to have
a baby, a Jewish baby,
in that place.
I have no regrets.
But then I think about
the beautiful daughters
I have and wonder if
that too would not have
been a wonderful child,
the one we slaughtered
that day in Münster,
in the hope of making
our own lives safe.
"Well, what could I do?
We couldn't have a baby
and run away from home
at the same time!"

IV.

"I had a dream," she said,
"just before we left
for America, and in the
dream, I was walking on
a very narrow footbridge
that was swaying from side
to side over a deep river
and had no railings, nothing
to hold on to. You were
in front of me and I had
my hands on your waist
and I said, close your
eyes, everything will
be all right. I wasn't afraid."

And she never even heard of
Rabbi Nachman who struggled

endlessly to find joy and
bring it to his suffering
people while trying to steer
clear of the abyss himself,
or that he taught that
all the world's a narrow bridge,
and the essential thing
is not to fear at all.
She knew it in her bones.

V.

"Sometimes," she says,
"sometimes, when I take
off my clothes in front
of the mirror and I see
my naked body and feel ashamed
I think of my poor mother
and how she had to do
that in front of all those
people, all doing the same
thing, and then I cry."

It's good that she can
focus on that part of
the horror, rather than the
shooting, the blood, the
asphyxiation in a mass
grave outside of Minsk.

"She was such a good person,
my mother. Once she saved
money to buy herself a
new winter coat and then
she gave it to a woman
who needed one more than
she did. 'I'll get along,'
she said.
She deserved better, don't
you think?"

I do. Everybody deserves better.

VI.

My mother would be happy
to wake up dead one morning.
"Don't you think it's enough?"
she asks me.
"I have had a long, good life.
Isn't it enough?"

"It's enough for you perhaps,
but not for us," I tell her.
"We can't get enough of you."

Not only that. We all want to
be like her. Amazing. Brave. And
cheerful, incredibly cheerful.

≈≈ *4/1/03*≈≈

Kadosh Kadosh

Blessed is life
and our small portion of it,
blessed the possibility
that lets us come to be
from microscopic specks
of cosmic dust, miracle-
making molecules of life

streaming from one source,
one supreme, solitary font
of being through which all beings
in the universe we know
are linked, connected, one
to another... blessed is the
One, the Source of life.

blessed is the division from one
into many, the holy sequence
that makes acorns into soaring oaks,
Einsteins and DaVincis from zygotic cells;
blessed are the things we can't explain
for they are God, and blessed too
the things we can explain,
for they are God as well.

≈≈ *8/8/03* ≈≈

If I Should Die Before I Wake

If I should die before I wake
I know no one my soul would take
nor would it flutter to the sky
to merge up there with God on high

for soul and God are mere conceits
designed for us as cosmic treats
to circumvent the truth that we
just can't comprehend the mystery
of human life upon this earth
and what -- if anything -- it's worth.

So when I die some night or day
and breathe my last without a say
I'm more than absolutely sure
my soul (which if it is, is pure)

will with my non-existent god
refuse to tread where angels trod
and rather stick real close to me
as I fade into eternity.

≈≈ 8/20/06 ≈≈

Maker of Peace

A lifetime ago, in that far-off place
where gossamer dreams turned to solid ash
my mother and I were children together

and we played and sang and made Shabbat
with that adorable grandfather of hers,
soaking in the words he chanted

and the tune of the *Oseh Shalom*
that he sang, wine glass raised
to the heavens, humbly asking for peace

from the One on High Who Wasn't Listening
so that what happened happened and no
Maker of Peace came along to save the day.

But as luck would have it, and we had it,
we grew old, and now, sometimes confused,
she calls me mom when she needs something

and if that fails to bring what she wants,
she cries out *Mutter, Mutter, Mutter,*
for the other mother, the one they killed

the one she never wept for, until now,
and then I hum to her that ancient song
whose lilting words, unwitting threnody,

even our enfeebled synapses can recall
so that the long-gone Opa Karl still
makes her smile and sing along in peace.

≈≈6/1/05≈≈

A Good Thing

We weren't looking for holiness.
Modern Jews, for whom the old rules
are suggestions, guideposts, and
sometimes obsolete recommendations,
we recognized no need for holiness
in our lives. We thought we'd share
traditions, eat ritual meals, teach
our children to be good Jews,
and even more important,
good citizens of the world,
without being "too religious"
for our tastes. And yet, and yet....
when we came together to share
our joys and our sorrows, when we
looked into each other's souls,
and learned to fill the spaces
between us all with love,
we found to our continuing surprise
that the holiness we never sought
was here, within ourselves
and one another.

Holiness has been around.
It's what Moses had in mind
at the beginning, before the word
fell into misuse and then disuse.
In the beginning, in the old days,
before the Holy Torah and the
Holy Temple were even in our heads,
it was he who saw what most cannot
and knew that holiness
was not in things, not even in words,
and yet most worth having.

When first he sweet-talked us,
coaxed us into leaving the land
of the death worshippers,
where -- bad as things were --
we did have meat and cucumbers
to eat when the day's work was done,

and led us into the wilderness
with barely a crumb, barely a drop,
to keep body and soul together,
he promised us
in the name of all that's sacred
we would find holiness out there,
and become a holy nation.

We fell for it, went along with him,
though we had more questions,
then as now, than answers.
Holiness? we asked him then,
and wonder now, with open hearts,
Whatever did he mean by that?
His answer was a set of rules for living,
rules that, he said, and some believed,
came straight from God.

The first were simple, allowing no killing,
no adultery, no coveting, No Other God
than the One we could not see,
the source of all from whom we gained
not only life and freedom but a
heavenly day of rest.
The hard rules came later, the detailed
prescriptions for order and for giving thanks
to the fount of holiness who would make us holy,
if only we played by the rules.

That's what he said, the man Moses,
the one who found his life's truth
within a burning bush, knew holiness
when he saw it, face to face, and knew
what was required to live holy lives.
He had few followers on that path.
Easier to follow him to the Jordan than
to holiness. We became wanderers.

Along the long way from then till now,
long after Hamidbar and after Babylon,
after Worms and Granada, after Berlin
and Nuremberg, and after Auschwitz,

the recipe for holiness was lost.
We forgot the concept, remembered
only that we were a people of the Book
whose rules and sacrifices set us apart
from all the others, and, more than anything,
we wanted not to be apart from all the others.
And so we left the rules for the old folk,
and for a while lived our lives as pagans,
thinking we were just fine. For a while.

What our lives were missing
we did not know
until we found it again.
Here. To our amazement,
the holiness we never sought was here,
within ourselves and one another.
And it was good.

≈≈*3/25/03*≈≈

Early Morning

Lying in bed, just opening my eyes
enough to see the gray morn peering in
searching inside for the sun's light

I think at first I must be dead,
so strangely tranquil do I feel
under the soft and downy cover
of early dawn,

I notice that I have no pulse,
I have no pulse: I must be dead,
that is my waking thought and so

I do a mental check of all my systems
not agonized but just routinely noting
my breathing's slow enough to miss,

the body reflected in the mirror
so still, so unmoving, I observe
objectively it looks like mine,

like me, but dead, and really,
I don't seem to care a whit
and can't decide

if I should breathe
or not, and lie in wait for
my pulse to start again. Or not.

And then, while I'm deciding,
an unrequisitioned breath
brings me to life.

≈≈1/31/05≈≈

Choose Life

In days of old when we placed
our choicest words of wisdom
in the mouths of oracles, or dreams,
or even in the Voice of God,
to give them strength and power
and force we thought they
wouldn't have if heard from us
(so modest were we then,
and yet so brazen,
so filled with holy chutzpah!)

it was then we say God spoke
the most important words
we'll ever hear: Choose Life,
I put before you life and death:
choose life. And yes, it's true,
still true, we have that choice,
that holy choice to make
each day we wake again to light
and find our breath still with us.

Hear me now, not God, but
me your friend who knows
the darkness,
saying straight to you:
choose life, this very moment,
not when you're looking
down from a mountain top
at harmony and peace
but when you look up and find
there is no light anywhere around
and all is blackness and despair,
when pain screams out
from every cell,

when honey tastes like poison on
your tongue, and your life's worth
less than the clothes you barely
manage to put on,
then, then,
choose life, and, more,
seek the treasure hiding from you,
and find just a tiny spark of joy.
It is our task, our holiest task,
to find the sparks of joy
always within our reach.

≈≈1/26/06≈≈

I Am What I Am

Ehyeh asher ehyeh
said God to Moses
in the only authorized
biography of either,
meaning, we think,
"I am what I am" or
"I'll be what I'll be,"
making no promises
and no excuses either
just what you see is
what you get.

Or he might have meant,
we can't be sure, the vagaries
of ancient Hebrew syntax
leave much in doubt,
he might have meant just
to foretell that he would always
be just what he'd always been,
not one bit more than that.

In Hebrew there is no future
tense so God spoke in
what's called Imperfect
of an act or state of being
not yet completed, continuing
on in its imperfect way.

But now, the myth complete,
ready to be filed away
for Goodness' sake,
we can say, in Truth:
Elohim haya asher haya:
God was what he was
whatever that was.

≈≈9/27/07≈≈

essays

essays

All Things Considered

My father at seventy-six was hale and hearty, although that description suggests a truck driver of a man and he was more of a rocking-chair-on-the-porch type, small and gentle and, by all appearances, totally meek and docile (though it goes without saying that appearances can be deceiving and I can remember more than one instance when, in the safe recesses of the third floor apartment that was my childhood home, I could hear him rant to my mother against the abuses of numberless absent oppressors who had treated him unfairly). He was aging well, suffering few of the diminutions that accompany the passing of years and was still as agile and amusing and lovable, I thought, as he had ever been.

When he and my mother flew in from California for my son's June wedding in St. Louis, however, he had less than his usual energy. He dozed a lot -- we thought medication he was taking for a chronic urinary condition was sedating him -- and spoke of a persistent heaviness in his abdomen that he had mentioned to his doctor more than once without finding satisfaction. Then, the day before the wedding, as the festivities were about to begin, there were blood clots in his urine. A local urologist medicated him and urged him to have a full kidney workup when he was back home. He didn't

essays

tell him what he knew.

Two weeks later, a California urologist performed tests that revealed a large mass on the left kidney. It was a malignancy, the doctor felt sure, but if it was restricted to the one kidney as he believed it to be, it could be removed without having a major impact on my dad's life. A nephrectomy was scheduled for the seventh of July. It was a Monday. Mom and I rose early and drove to the hospital to send Dad off to surgery. He was happy to see me; I had just flown in the night before. He seemed perfectly carefree. Leaning against the sink of his little lavatory, clad in his own blue pajamas, he was shaving, slowly, slowly, the way he always did everything, as if he had all the time in the world. He was chatty and very optimistic about the outcome of the surgery, in large part because he had under-stood the doctor to have told him that "ninety to ninety-five per cent of tumors such as this are not malignant!"

When around noon an attendant came to roll him away to the operating room, Dad was still telling us, in his deliberate and painstaking fashion, a hyperdetailed story about his Uncle Moses who had fled Germany for South Africa long before and who, he said, was "ninety-two or maybe ninety-three years ....well, no...I think he was ninety-two years old...I'm sure he was ninety-two....when he died." My father always wanted to get every detail right, in his stories as in life.

We rode down in the elevator with him as far as the lobby, he smiling, chatting, all the way. We wished him well and let him go. We didn't think to say good-bye. We sat then and waited, as instructed -- it was to be three to four hours before we could expect to hear -- and then waited and waited again. At four an attendant came out to tell us there had been a delay; the operation would take a bit longer. At 5:30, the surgeon himself appeared, still in his green surgical scrubs, to give us his account of the protracted surgery.

He said that he had removed a mass the size of a grapefruit along with the entire left kidney, had sent sections and lymph nodes to the pathology lab for examination, and had every confidence that the cancer had been wholly encapsulated, with no spread whatsoever of malignancy outside the affected left kidney.

That was good. Before our hopes could soar too high, he told us the rest, the unexpected part: just as he and his surgical assistant were preparing to fold up the kidney for removal (yes, that's what he said, "fold up the kidney"), he noted that the renal artery leading from the aorta to the right kidney had been severed. Which is to say, though he did not say it at the time, that he had removed the wrong kidney, the right, healthy kidney, because he thought it was the left kidney. And then, when he realized what had gone wrong, that the unhealthy kidney was still in place and the good one was detached, he was astounded and amazed.

Not sure how such a thing could have happened, (to him, of all people!) he had hurriedly called in a vascular surgeon to consult and then to lead in the resectioning and reattachment of the severed artery. The additional two hours expended on this corrective surgery brought to a total of three hours the length of time for which the remaining, "good" kidney was deprived of blood flow. A long, long time. Kidneys need blood to function. So it was immediately question-able whether my dad would survive this trauma.

We were hopeful. We refused to entertain the notion that he would not come home again. When we first saw him post-operatively, we were pleased with the way he looked, wholly tranquil and uncomplaining. He smiled and managed to say that "this place is very relaxing" and later in the day to ask "Did they take it all out?" We were encouraged, but very briefly, for he never spoke again. His last words stayed with us, soothing us as his situation spiraled rapidly downwards.

essays

His vital signs destabilized, his traumatized kidney failed, and he passed into a comatose state during which countless specialists conferred and labored, hard, to bring his poor insulted body back to life.

Their efforts failed. Nine long roller coaster days after the botched surgery, he died. We had given a directive to withhold heroic measures in case of breathing or cardiac arrest, and when the nephrologist told us that the moment had come, that dialysis was no longer possible without further surgery, that there was a good chance of permanent cerebral damage after so many days of coma, we agreed to let him slip away. They stopped the dialysis. There was cardiac arrest, and he died.

We were sad, incredibly sad, but we weren't angry.

II.

The anger came later, when the death certificate arrived. It was delayed by an official investigation initiated by the county coroner's office, of which I first heard from the funeral director, right before the funeral service began. Leaning across the front pew in his somber black suit, looking appropriately sympathetic, he asked whether Dad had had a fall or some other accident at the hospital. He was just wondering, he said, because somebody official was not satisfied with the cause of death given on the hospital's report of the death and had authorized an investigation into the death.

"I wouldn't expect much from such an investigation," I said.

"You'd be surprised what they can find out," the funeral director said from long experience. He was right; I was.

The following day, a deputy coroner explained that the office was looking into "a gray area" that demanded explication. Without mentioning that such investigations are normal procedures pursuant to surgical accidents, she told me that the causes of death listed on the hospital death report (which causes included renal failure) merited investigation. The necessary examination of tissue would continue for weeks; the death certificate could be delayed for up to eight weeks. And it was.

What the death certificate said when I finally had it in my hand made me crazy. After eight weeks of delay, after an autopsy demanded by the state, after microscopic examinations and other investigations, the legal cause of death had become "Occlusion, left coronary artery, due to, or as a consequence of arteriosclerotic cardiovascular disease".

That there was no mention of the surgical mishap was shocking but not a total surprise. In mid-August the deputy had telephoned to inform me of the results of the investigation. In essence, she told me that my father's body had shown considerable evidence of arteriosclerosis, that the corrective surgery had been done superbly, and, imagine this, that he would have died even if he had not had the surgery.

I couldn't believe my ears. I remember this conversation as if it were yesterday though now it is twenty years past. I remember how I stood there, frozen in the corner of my family room in St. Louis County, holding the phone away from my head for a moment to check whether it was real or some apparition from outer space, while this California person was mumbling gibberish to me from Orange County.

"What?" I sputtered at last. "What?! My father would have died anyway? When? What day? Is there a crystal ball in your office?"

Well-trained in the arts of bureaucratic relations, she remained polite in response to my outburst. She just wanted me to know they were doing everything to

essays

expedite the investigation pursuant to state regulations, she said. And that the death certificate would publish the official determination of the coroner's office.

So when it finally arrived, the death certificate delivered the authoritative declaration of the state that my father, who had been such a good sport about the surgery, whose faith in modern medicine had persisted beyond the doomed operation, whose body had been examined, dissected, explored, transfused, dialyzed, peered into and finally mutilated and violated in the name of some greater truth, had died of heart disease!

Now I was ready to rant. In his honor, in his memory, I was ready to take on the State of California. We are believers in compassion in our family and were quite willing to extend that compassion to the unfortunate surgeon whose momentary misperception, by his own admission to us, led to my father's death. We knew from conversations with him that he was deeply troubled by the lamentable occurrence and we had no desire to add to his pain. We could understand that people make mistakes and had rejected out of hand the suggestion often made to us that we file suit for damages against him and/or the hospital.

But the State of California was another beast altogether. Who did they think they were? On receipt of the death certificate, I wrote to the Sheriff-Coroner of Orange County as if I were a half-mad character in a Bellow novel.

Dear Mr. Gates:

As you will note by the letterhead, I am not a resident of California so perhaps I may be forgiven if I do not understand the official actions that followed the death of my father, above named, last July. I direct my questions to you since it was your office that instigated and carried out the questionable actions.........

essays

Following a handy synopsis of the events as they unfolded, I recited the finding on the death certificate and the supporting remarks of the deputy in the August conversation to the effect that the corrective surgery had been done admirably, that my father's body evidenced considerable heart damage and that he would have died even if he had not had the surgery. And then I restarted on the vitriol:

> Now I respectfully submit, esteemed Sir, that even before your staff became involved in my family affairs, I was aware that my father was not immortal. Perhaps that is what made it possible for me to accept his death even though it came as the result of an unfortunate surgical misjudgment.
>
> I cannot, however, accept an official whitewash as the necessary consequence. I can see no reasonable explanation for the findings of your staff who seem intent on proving that my father never had kidneys, let alone a tragic accident involving them. His death was the direct result of the termination of dialysis, dialysis which he would not have required had the operation proceeded normally. To ascribe the death to a coronary occlusion rather than to the failure to revitalize a kidney wounded as the result of an erroneously severed renal artery is, I very much suspect, intentionally deceptive.
>
> Please feel free to combat my suspicions by explaining to me, if you can:
> - the reason for removing renal failure from the official cause of death;
> - the reason for your staff's emphasis on the 'wonderful job' done with respect to the corrective surgery while negating the significance of the accident itself;
> - the interest your office has in protecting a

essays

fine hospital like St. X and the medical professionals who serve there from the truth.

Sincerely yours, etc.......

Perhaps no right-minded person would expect a favorable response to such a disrespectful letter, but I did nonetheless receive one. After a personal call from the Sheriff-Coroner begging for my patience while they reconsidered, I received in due time a letter from him detailing the results of a review of the entire matter. A new character had entered the drama, a forensic pathologist other than the Dr. Y who had performed the autopsy and signed off on the death certificate. This doctor amended the death certificate to include, as cause of death,

"Acute renal insufficiency, Tubular necrosis, Surgical laceration, right renal artery, and Other conditions: adenocarcinoma, left kidney, operated..."

He also reported having observed tubular regeneration, which is to say healing, taking place in areas of the remaining kidney but "the insult or embarrassment was too severe and resulted in the death of your father."

And that's the end of the story. There was a mistake in the operating room followed by a mistake in the coroner's department. So said the Sheriff-Coroner in his letter, responding gently to the harsh innuendos contained in my letter to him:

Be assured that there was no effort to cover up or be deceptive. There simply was an error in medical judgment by the original examining pathologist and we apologize.
Dr. Y is no longer on our staff.

I was beside myself with joy that my ranting had paid off and the truth had won out. It was all, in the realm of the possible, that I wanted.

III.

There was not a lot of weeping around our house when my father died, not because we didn't love him and want him around forever because we did, but because of a mild neurotic streak, intensified by the events of the last century, which afflicts our family. We just don't deal with death in any kind of a normal way. If I had been as aware of this then, maybe I would not have been as astounded as I was, her comments freezing my mouth open, when just hours after we slipped his remains into the ground, my mother said to the assembled family members, "I think he was really lucky. I think that my guardian angel must have been watching over Daddy."

Silence fell with a thud into the little room when she said that. With our mouths agape, we one and all tried to imagine her reasoning. Where did she see the beneficial effect of her guardian angel? In the cancer? in the aborted surgery? In the nine days of unrelenting but finally futile struggle against the Angel of Death, hovering, hovering over his comatose body? Where? Where?

"He never knew he had cancer," she said. "He would have been afraid of cancer, and he died without knowing he had it. I know that was my guardian angel at work."

I resisted the impulse to laugh out loud. My mother can find good luck anywhere and can barely see the clouds for the silver linings. Denial is her middle name. We kid her about this, but the kind of denial skills she demonstrated in turning her tragic loss into a miracle on the very day of the funeral, without batting an eyelash or shedding one tear, shows what an under-appreciated coping strategy denial can be. It is one that my mother came by honestly.

essays

Some forty years before my dad's also premature death, soon after we had the good luck to escape from a homeland that had taken on the mission of purifying itself of our kind, my mother's relatives (my father's too) were systematically murdered by the Nazis. But while the mass killing was orderly and efficient, the system failed to provide for notification of the abruptly bereaved, who were forced to infer the deaths of their loved ones from the spate of devastating news emanating from that part of the world.

My mother never had a chance to grieve. She worried, she hoped, and she went on living. By the time the official government records confirmed that on November 8, 1941, her beloved parents had been transported (yes, that's the innocent word the City of Hamburg used in its official transcript of the horrific events, a weightless word now burdened with heavy images of pistol-pointing goosestepping brutes whipping ragged people forward on bloodied feet, and cattle cars packed like sardine cans with living, breathing human beings smashed against one another and against corpses lacking space in which to fall, and images of faces, faces and more faces stripped of everything but anguish and horror), transported, that is, across all Europe to the frozen ground around Minsk, Russia, there to be forced alongside numberless co-religionists and relatives to dig their own mass grave, it was too late for tears. By that time so many millions of innocents were known to be dead, she could no longer weep for just two.

In reaction to the bitter news from Hamburg, exacerbated by subsequent news of similar extermi-nations of my third grandparent and of numerous aunts, uncles and cousins, at least some of us developed a neurotic acceptance of death as remediation, as a welcome end to pain and suffering. So awful, so precise, was our imagining of the events that preceded the killings of our family members that our only solace came from the fact that death had ended their tortures

essays

and brought them peace.

We came over the years to generalize this observation, to see death as a desired salvation from all suffering within our frame of reference. And to see death in bed, in a hospital bed, at that, as an ending much to be envied. It became over time harder and harder to express sympathy to acquaintances who had lost loved ones to mortal illness, the relatively antiseptic ending of those lives coming in rough contrast to the spectral memory, always in our minds, of the unkind deaths suffered by the six million. We came to apprehend a good death as a reward to be savored, appreciated.

Unnatural or not, pathological or not, it was logically consistent for us to treat our own losses in the same analytical way, accepting death without much grief. We knew, after all, no other way than the one we had fallen into as a consequence, though an indirect consequence, of the destiny that had befallen us. Lucky enough to evade the exterminators and unlucky enough to have lost loved ones, we managed to have the Holocaust always in our heads.

Knowing this, I should have seen my mother's gratitude to her guardian angel as right on target. Because we had each established long ago, independently, without consulting one another, that death may in some instances be preferable to suffering. The fear of suffering supplants the fear of death in those of us who just can't bear even the idea of pain. So painful is the consciousness, or even the suspicion, that someone is suffering that we find ourselves praying for death, welcoming death, to bring the suffering to an end. Often, we give up too soon, before the person suffering has thought of giving up.

It is possible that we let my father go too soon. In our readiness to protect him from suffering, perhaps we didn't fight hard enough to extend his life. Of course, I wonder about this. But I saw him once, once during

essays

those nine days of subhuman, expressionless, mechanically supported existence, when his face briefly contorted and he uttered a growling sound from some primitive brain center I hadn't known existed to express a momentary discomfort or pain or unhappiness or God-knows-what and in that instant, before he fell back into bland and silent disaffection, I glimpsed the chance that he might continue to live with diminished capacity and I knew, in that same micro-instant, what end he would wish for himself.

I knew because he shared my obsession. "Not a day goes by that I don't think of them," my father said wistfully not long before the surgery. He was stand-ing in my kitchen then, looking forward to the wedding he had come to witness but reflecting on the fate of my martyred grandparents.

It was forty years since they'd been prodded from their beds at gunpoint, then pushed and shoved across all Europe so they could die slow and grue-some deaths on frigid Russian steppes, and he was still trying to figure it out. He looked sad and pensive. And said no more.

It was all I ever heard him say about it. In forty years of searching, he had not found the words to express all that festered in his heart and head. There are of course no words that could convey it all: the painfilled memories of loss, the lingering thorny bitterness of knowing what he knew, and how little he could do about it, the anguish and despair and fear of countless sleepless nights and the hopelessness and guilt that numbed the days, and even the gratitude, the guilty gratitude for surviving and living well. Why me? the survivor's perennial fixation was deeply rooted in his brain. Why should I be so fortunate when so many were slaughtered?

I can't be sure, of course, but I suspect that, had he had, as he lay dying, consciousness and intellectual capacity beyond that of the dog brain I witnessed crying

essays

out, he would have compared his end to those other deaths of which he knew in a dispassionate fashion. All things considered (and he would have considered all things), my father would have thought himself a lucky man, surgical accident or no surgical accident.

At least, of this I am sure: he died without protracted pain, and in bed. In our family, such a death still counts as a blessing.

≈≈6/11/2003≈≈

essays

Too Good To Be True
an annotated life story

I swear to tell the truth, the whole truth, and nothing but the truth, so help me God. This is what I would say with respect to the story I am about to share with you were I not so thoroughly committed to truthfulness. I am only too aware that this oath, on which we rely to hold witnesses to a high standard of honor in courts of law, makes unwilling perjurers of them all. For who can know the whole truth, and who can tell it? For that matter, what lawyer would allow it to be told, what jury could sit still for all it?

I could never swear to tell the whole truth, even if the request were limited to the truth that is known to me. There is always one other aspect to explore after we have told it all, one additional explanation of what we mean by reference to a certain concept, one additional fact that is peripherally related and really should be mentioned, one additional interpretation of what we or others have said or thought we or others said at the moment we or they were saying it. And that is with regard to ordinary matters.

Writing truth about the Holocaust is even more problematic. It is a literary minefield that tolerates fiction badly but puts immense obstacles in the path of truthfulness. Even with the purest of aims, Holocaust writing is prone to distortion by bias, faulty memories, and intentional and unintentional simplifications and

essays

misinterpretations of facts. Still, the stories must be told so that we can assemble the truth, such as it is, from the individual shards into which civilized life was broken during that terrible time. Because I am fervently dedicated to the truth and to truth telling, even when it is not politic to be so, even when it may offend, even when it is not complete, I risk offering here a survivor's tale which may sound too good to be true, but is true, as true as I can make it. At least now. This moment.

The story, which sounds too good to be true, begins when I met Ilse Koster[1] at a retirement center in Laguna Hills, California, where she lives in an apartment a floor above that of my mother. My mother, who knows everyone who lives at Villa Valencia, has urged me to meet the woman and hear the remarkable tale she had to tell. It is a cause for some wonderment to me that my mother, who does not think about the Holocaust for fear of psychic disintegration,[2] has begged me, who cannot stop thinking about it, for related reasons, to have this encounter. But Mom was right. I needed to meet this woman. A vivacious octogenarian, pleasant and engaging, there is nothing in her appearance or manner to suggest that she has experienced the god-awful horror of the Nazi concentration and extermination camps. She smiles a lot[3] even

---

1   It is her real name. This story is true, as true as it can be. Haven't I convinced you of that?

2   Though she does not admit this, or even know this to be true. She has chosen not to talk about the Holocaust, or think about its effects on her life. What good does it do, she asks, to think about so much sadness? She is not as complex as I, she always says if I reveal my ongoing obsession. She likes to be happy, she says, and who would begrudge her that? I am sometimes envious of her ability to put things out of mind that threaten her peace of mind.

3   She smiles a lot but it is strange how much the smile echoes the smile that I routinely saw on the face of my Aunt Hannah after she came out of the camp in which she lost the love of her life, her husband Davis. It was an odd lip-extend-

while she relates her gruesome experiences.

One afternoon, the three of us had tea in Mom's apartment. "Tell her," my mother said to Ilse, with more enthusiasm than I would have expected, "tell her about your escapes."

"Mom," I said, "let me do this. OK?" And I slipped into my interviewer role, tape recorder at the ready.

Q: So, start at the beginning. Tell us your story.

"*Ja.* I started life as Ilse Scharff in Posen, now Poland. I was born on November 25, 1913. I was born into a middle class Jewish family. So.[4] There was my mother and father and two brothers, and we lived together in a nice house, comfortable and happy. My parents had a distribution center for beer and mineral waters and did quite well. Posen was then part of Germany but after the First World War it became part of Poland.

"Under the Poles, Posen was no longer a good place for us. My father, he had fought as a German officer, so when the War ended, some Polish soldiers came to

---

ing smile that bravely displayed her teeth but which also featured a tiny cynical upturn at the corner of the mouth that always had me wondering what she would say about her experiences if one could persuade her to speak about them. When brave souls in her presence broached the topic of the Holocaust in general, the smile filled her face, her eyes sparkled, as if in delight that she was outsmarting us all as she remained silent. In fifty years, she never revealed her secrets. The twisted smile hid them from view.

4 How easily she says this. What a frightening, hair-raising situation this must have been, she doesn't say, as if she has forgotten the details or can't admit to being scared half out of her wits. As I would have been, I know, having often pictured myself in the same situation, although I wasn't, ever, close to such a thing; nothing really happened to me. I was totally safe, having the good fortune to make a legal escape from that hell on earth with both my mother and father before any one of us was incarcerated or subjected to tortures of the sort that befell many of those dearest to us.

our house right away to make trouble. I don't know if they thought we were spies for Germany or what. They didn't hurt us but they opened all the cabinets and looked under the floorboards to see what we were hiding, looking for guns and grenades and God-only-knows-what.

"They left the house a total mess, [5] and in the moment they left, my father decided that we had to get out. And we did, as quickly as possible. I was about five when we left Poland and moved across the border to Brieg in Germany, where my parents started a chocolate factory. That is where I got my sweet tooth. I still love chocolate. *Ja*. But my father soon got very ill with diabetes and then tuberculosis and was for a long time in a sanatorium far from home. This was expensive care which used up pretty much all the money the family had, but anyway he died when I was about 16 years old. The rest of us moved to Berlin.

"Oh, I loved Berlin. It was such a beautiful city and I was a girl with lots of energy. I took some secretarial courses and worked at a number of jobs with a variety of businesses. But then Hitler came to power and Jews could no longer work for Aryans, so I found a good job as a secretary with the Jewish cultural society. It was at this job that I first came close to being interned.

"That was about the time I got married too. I met my husband at a New Year's Eve dance. for Jews. Of

---

5 I look at my mother to check for a sign of recognition at this point of the story but there is none, even though what Ilse describes is exactly how the Nazis left our house in Bünde on the night of November 8, 1938, in the opening salvo of Germany's War Against the Jews. Although she and I were away that night, we know from my father's account what transpired and have the image clearly imprinted onto our memories. We know what happened in Bünde that night as well as what happened in Hamburg, which was no carnival either. Or perhaps it was, for those brutes who reveled in the trashing of synagogues and who caroused to the sound of shattering glass falling to the earth of that beautiful city which had, prior to that day, been home to Jews for happy centuries after the expulsion from Iberia.

≈148≈

course, only for Jews. It was not any longer permitted for Jews to mingle with Aryans. His name was -- I can hardly remember, I have had so many men since then -- it was, uh, Bernard Levy." She laughs heartily and continues.

"I should not say this, I really shouldn't, but one of my colleagues at this job actually turned me in, to be taken to the concentration camp."

Q: Why shouldn't you say this?

"Because it is such a *Schande*, a shame! For him! to do such a terrible thing![6] Anyway, one day in 1941, this man who worked alongside me came up to me with a Gestapo officer at his side and told me to come along. He was Jewish, this guy. I hate to tell you this[7] but some people thought they would save their own lives if they helped the Gestapo with their searches. They would go out and catch other Jews and bring them into the *Sammellager*, the collection center, to be sent away. The Gestapo wanted Jewish people, and so they brought them Jewish people, in order to save their own lives. Can you imagine?

"So I said to this traitor, this Judas person, 'I am not going without my husband.' When he insisted, I thought quickly and said, 'You know, I am supposed to

---

6 I am confused at first, wondering who it is that she thinks she is betraying but then realize that she is betraying her own standard of behavior. She is actually embarrassed that a human being, and a Jew at that, could act in such a cavalier fashion, but is disinclined to say bad things about people, even if they are true. She is ashamed to say the truth, here and elsewhere in the interview, because the truth reflects so badly on others, and speaking the truth about them reflects badly on her. She has a very stringent moral code.

7 There is this factor as well: sweet and caring by nature, she doesn't want to be the bearer of bad news, does not wish to contaminate my world view, not knowing that my world view was long ago contaminated by the abstract knowledge of what she and millions of others were forced to endure.

have a crown put on a tooth today. Would you let me, please, just go across the street and get the dentist to do it before I go with you?' I guess he was ashamed to say no so he let me do it. I ran to the dentist but I never went back home again. Instead, I found my way through back streets to a friend's house. I knew my way around. And that was my first escape.

"I called my mother and told her to warn my husband not to go home, he should join me instead at my friend's house. She did that and we stayed there for a few days. Later we went back to our apartment; I even went back to my job. My so-called colleague was gone by then. In the meantime,[8] the *Jüdisches Kulturbund* came under the direction of the Gestapo. I kept going to work every day, hoping for the best. But the Gestapo came to the house one day and picked us up, marching my husband and me and lots of others to the *Grosser Hamburger Strasse*, where they were collecting Jews.[9]

---

8   There must have been a forgotten lapse of time between her running off to avoid internment and her return to the site, although in her telling it is just a day or two. This seems to be an instance of innocent forgetting. People forget things, even if they are less than 86 years old. Certainly I forget things, and not always for deep psychological reasons. Sometimes we just cannot remember, perhaps for physiological reasons -- an insufficiency of nerve endings, a shortage of electricity in the brain, some day we will know these things with a certainty -- the actual sequence of events we have witnessed. Nonetheless, I cannot help wondering whether, in her recounting, she has actually forgotten the other periods of time that she does not describe, the intervals between the adventures and the escapes, when the terrible things happened.

9 Her statement makes me think of the terror that my mother's parents must have felt when they were summoned at their Hamburg apartment in November 1941, my Opa carrying the leather satchel he had filled with their absolute necessities and kept waiting at the door so that, when the inevitable knock came, they could respectfully, submissively, follow the instructions barked at them. They were such good citizens, my grandparents. They could only

"That same day, my husband got very sick, and it was a good thing. The Gestapo took him to the Jewish hospital, the *Jüdisches Krankenhaus*, with diphtheria. While he was kept there, I was put to work in a sewing room where I was made to sew clothes for people picked up from their workplaces who didn't have anything appropriate to wear. Why we had to do that I still don't know because as soon as you got to the concentration camp they took everything -- all your clothes and everything else -- away from you!

"Then, when he got better and came out from the hospital, I was lucky: I got diphtheria and that saved us for a year in Berlin in the *Sammellager*. The others, who were healthy, got sent on to terrible places where most people died. But they could not send us away with the diphtheria because it was too contagious. They knew enough science to want to avoid epidemics. So, in a way, that was another escape. It was 1942.

"Eventually, we were taken to the concentration camps: Theresienstadt[10], Auschwitz, Gross Rosen: my husband and I both but never together, always separated. In Auschwitz I could still see him occasionally but not any more later. Then he went on to Sachsenhausen too but I didn't.

"First we were in Theresienstadt, the model camp, the one they kept just to show visiting diplomats how well prisoners were treated. It was the propaganda camp

---

follow orders, and hope for the best, which they deserved but certainly did not get. We don't know if they were among the lucky ones to be shot before they were buried in the mass grave just outside of Minsk that they were forced to dig for themselves and all their colleagues in anguish.

10 She drops the name of this camp into the ferment already bubbling in my brain. Theresienstadt, where my father's father lingered for months, writing us plaintive semi-hopeful letters articulating his wishes for survival, before he died, at the hands of the Nazis, in November 1942. The Germans issued a death certificate which was later delivered to us. They had respect for civilities there, it being the model camp.

and sometimes, rarely, we did have good treatment.

"For dinner one night they gave us dumplings with plums inside; that was so good. And I met my mother there, and that was good[11] but she later died in transport to Auschwitz.

"With work I was lucky;[12] they needed someone at a factory. I don't really know what they made there but when they saw I had worked as secretary, they took me to do office work. only filing papers so it was actually not too bad for me.

"We were there for 4, 5, months and then were moved to Auschwitz. There we worked at making something for bombs. We braided these things by hand that you use to light up bombs. We lived in bunks, the men and women separately, of course, packed like sardines, eight people in one bunk, and I was on the third one up. The bunks were just boards, not beds, and no sheets, no mattresses. They figured, naturally, what would Jews need such comforts for?[13]

---

11 Note how her mind works. She has said nothing negative about the treatment she received but recalls two good things: the plum dumplings and seeing her mother for the last time. She accentuates the positive, pushes aside the negative and manages to remember, only the good stuff in Hell.

12 Lucky? You would think no one has ever been so lucky. But luck is where you find it, and she found it, everywhere: the diphtheria, the kind of work she was assigned, the persons who helped her, all were signs of good fortune. The fact that she lives to tell the tale is proof that she is right in this assessment. Still, I cannot help but ask the "glass half empty" question of the trained pessimist, how lucky is someone who has had to survive the rigors of Auschwitz? while others worried about getting into the right schools, or what to serve their families for dinner?

13 The ironic tone she employs here is the closest she comes to condemning the harsh treatment she has witnessed, and experienced, choosing not to give voice to the cruel details of everyday life in the camps.

"It was bad there. You didn't get much to eat. You couldn't go to the washroom when you wanted to but only when they said you could go which was very bad because most of the people got diarrhea. You had no combs, no brushes, no toothbrushes; you could not wash yourself, you didn't have anything to wash yourself with.

"You could not comb your hair; most of the time, they shaved the heads anyway. They had to; we had lice. The first time I had them, I cried and cried. Before we moved on to the new camp, we had to turn in all our clothes and get new ones so we would not take the lice with us. Ja. The Germans worried about lice. For us they did not have enough time any more to shave the whole head so they just shaved a row in the middle. We were lucky in one sense: we did not have any mirrors to see ourselves in. We did not know how bad we looked.

"You had to get up in the morning at 3 o'clock for roll call, to be counted, before you went to work. Of course, they used force if they felt like it, if they did not like someone they would stab them with a knife. *Ja.*

"I was there, in Auschwitz, for a year, maybe...and I collected recipes.[14] There were people there from Hungary and they are wonderful cooks and they told the recipes to me and I wrote them down. I planned to write a cookbook when I came out but we left in a hurry and I could not take the papers with me when they moved me to Gross Rosen, a camp near Frankfurt. And when we got there, the officer told us right away that before us there were 600 Jews there and now they are all dead because they all died from poisoning. It was nice of him to tell us that so I knew I

---

14 Recipes? I know that people in dire circumstances must find a purpose for continuing but can't help feeling awe of such clear thinking, such creativity. Could I have been so clear-headed, so courageous? Saving recipes when there is nothing to cook and nothing to eat is a Sysyphean task. An enviable talent, this capacity to find optimistically charged projects *in extremis*.

had to escape sooner or later.

"Here we had to work with...we had to make bombs, and that powder you use for the bombs -- they call that SH salt or something -- affects people working with it, it affects their livers so they go crazy and they don't really know what they are doing. I heard that it's a terrible thing; that the workers would think they have food poisoning when they really had something much much worse, so I said to myself, whenever I feel like I have food poisoning, I will know it is time to leave.

"The supervisors were given protective masks to wear and got milk as an antidote, but we didn't, of course. So I worked with the stuff every day and every evening when I came home, I looked like a silver statue because that powder is like aluminum dust that gets all over you. I took showers to get the dust off but I said to my girlfriend, 'You know, whenever I see that I don't feel right, I will not think it is food poisoning, I will know it is time to go.' And we prepared for that for a long time.

"They had electric fences around the camp but whenever there was an air raid and the bombers came from America, they turned off the power and they all went into the bunker. And without the lights on, it was dark and we could work in safety. We dug a hole under the fence with our hands. Every time there was a blackout, we dug. Thank Heaven[15] , the bombers came often enough so we could finish the digging. We covered the hole nicely so no one would detect it."

Q: Did you have any digging tools to work with?

"No tools besides our hands but we were lucky to get some implements for sewing. Sometimes our supervisor would bring me things, a scissors and a needle, sometimes they were nice that way. Anyway,

---

15   I myself could never use that expression, even though I have much more to be thankful for. But she easily thanks Heaven for her good fortune as if she actually believes that divine intervention had saved her.   As if Heaven cared about human beings.

≈154≈

when we first got there and the Nazi gave that nice speech about the 600 Jews who'd died there, I got mad and said, 'Listen, we don't have anything to wear! In Auschwitz, they only left us with these short little outfits and we cannot work like this in the cold.' And he said, 'Come to me after the meeting is over and I will give you things.' He was nice, gave us gray suits to wear and said, 'Whenever you need something, come to me... "You want more food for your people there, come to me."[16] And he let me come and collect leftover food, at nine or ten in the evening, when the Germans were finished eating.

"Anyway, it was with his special gift of needles that I managed to make our get-away outfits. We had been given a blanket to cover ourselves with at night. That blanket I cut and sewed into pants for me and for my girlfriend. And we all got coats because it was very cold in Frankfurt and the coats, thank Heaven, were very long so I could cut off the excess and use that for other purposes. See, the backs of the coats had panels with stripes across them, stripes like our uniforms, you know, so that people could see right away we were prisoners. So I made some panels out of the extra coat material to cover the stripes nicely up and sewed them on and sort of basted the striped panels over them until we were ready.

"Finally the day came when I did not feel well and knew we had to leave. I told my friend and others too but no one wanted to go with us; they were afraid. I said, 'Of what? what else can happen worse?' But people are funny."[17]

---

16 Whatever favors she was required to offer in exchange are no longer part of the story, if there were such favors, if they were ever part of the story. Whatever terrible experiments she was subjected to in the name of Germanic science, if there were such experiments, do not come to mind in her telling, or are not told. And I do not ask. Nor do I ask her why she had no children.

17 People are certainly funny but the discovery that prisoners in a concentration camp, where punishment without reason is the norm, might be too fearful to undertake risky

Q: Yes, but you were perhaps more brave.

"No. I don't think so. We were young; it was an adventure. We did not have much to lose. When we were ready, we waited until I could pick up the leftovers I had been summoned by my officer friend to get, and it was ten o'clock before we dug our way out. Like two dogs, we climbed out underneath the fence, through the tunnel we had prepared for just such a moment.

"We walked, with no idea where we were going, and met a Russian in a horse and buggy who gave us a ride. By midnight we were in Frankfurt. It was January 1945 by then, and everything was already upside down, trains didn't run any more. We hoped to go to a town where my girl friend had a friend who maybe could give us some clothes.

"The first thing that happened in Frankfurt was that some policemen stopped us and we got scared but they only said if we wanted to sleep somewhere, they had a place where we could go but we said no, we want to go to so-and-so but there is no train going there and as we are saying that we want to walk to this town, like a miracle, a man came up from nowhere and said,'I heard you say where you want to go. I have to go there too. Do you want to follow me? because I know a shortcut through the quicksand. You have to follow me exactly, one after the other, don't go the right, and don't go to the left.' And we did it. We followed him just as he said. We didn't have any choice and we made it. It really was unbelievable how he appeared out of the darkness, like an angel, and then led us safely out of town.

"When we finally came to the friend's house, she took one look and almost fainted. 'Oh my gosh,' she cried, 'you come from the concentration camp. I will give you real fast some things to wear but my husband is an SS

---

behavior certainly does not come as a surprise to those of us who have known fear. And there is nothing funny in contemplating what happened to those of her companions who decided to avoid the risk of escaping with her.

Obersturmbahnfürer and he will be home soon.'

"We just had time to get some things to wear and run off. We wanted to get to Löbau where my girlfriend's mother ran a butcher shop. Maybe we could get some meat there. My friend sent me to go alone and I was thinking to myself how to handle this when I stopped to get something to eat. And there was a man sitting alone -- I am always lucky with men -- and he said, 'Do you mind if I sit with you?' and I said no. He told me that in his little village, all the people were already gone, evacuated in advance of the Russians' arrival, and he was alone in a big house and didn't really know what to do with it.

"And I said, 'You know, I have an idea. My girlfriend and I don't know where to live, we left Poland a long time ago, we lost everything, maybe we can take care of your house for you.' So we had a place to stay for a while. He had a bike I could use to get to her mother, who was maybe an hour's ride away. I rode there; the mother was very happy to hear that her daughter was alive and we got sausages from her that we could sell.

"This man was wonderful to us, really like a saint. He even went for us to Czechoslovakia, I don't know how he did it, to get material for us to make ourselves some clothes. And he let me work for him; I became his secretary and it was marvelous. I was able to fill out all my own papers in any way I wanted, and for my girlfriend. She did the housework, and I worked as a secretary.

"Later on, I went to Berlin to see if I could find out what happened to my mother and brothers. I was sitting at the railroad station when there was an air raid. I was so tired I fell asleep. When I woke up someone asked me how I could sleep during a raid like that. I couldn't tell him what I had been through.

"*Ja.* I went through a lot. But I was lucky, always lucky.[18] the way all kinds of people were good to me

---

18 Perhaps she is protecting me again, protecting me from that knowledge that she must live with but which no hu-

who weren't even Jewish."

Q: What does being Jewish mean to you now?

"I know I am Jewish. I won't change that. But it is not important. To me it is only the people that count, if they are good or bad or things like that. Don't forget, wherever I was there were always non-Jewish people who tried to help me, so to me as long as people are good, that is all that matters."

Q: What about God?

"Ah. Yes. What about God? I really don't know. You know what is strange? Whenever I escaped, from one place or another, and someone came to help me, I always thought, 'This is a miracle,' and it was a miracle but that is all I can say. More than that I cannot say although I would really like to know myself...what is going on in the world.

"I would really like to know....how everything happens... how the world is directed....and from where and.... I don't know.....*Ja*. I have always wanted to know that."

≈≈

Ilse Koster died shortly after this interview was completed. I barely knew her and yet was greatly saddened by her death. In the brief time we had together, she entranced me with her ability to put the Holocaust behind her, to transcend the memory of every cruelty, every pain, every moment of suffering and pain, with an incredible purity of heart.

That she was able to look back without anger or guilt was in itself amazing. That she was able to look

---

man being deserves to have. Or perhaps she is protecting herself. Yes, I know that is a possibility. If her story is true, who would quarrel with her right to defend herself against its continuing ravages by leaving things out? by forgetting, with intent, like my mother who can in fact forget there is evil in the world, if she puts her mind to it?

back as a witness who saw not the horror but the goodness she found along the way is what left me speechless. Hearing her tell her tale evoked a rush of unprecedented hope that human beings may be intrinsically better than events of the twentieth century led us to believe. If recent history taught that the human capacity for cruelty is infinite, and it did, it is encouraging (in the original courage-giving sense of the word) to speculate that there may also be no limit to the goodness of which we are, as a species, capable.

Even if that ideal sounds for the moment too good to be true, it is certainly not unrealistic to hope, pray, and almost believe that our children, or even our children's children, will one day find that it is not beyond human capacity to make the world a better place for all by connecting with that infinite goodness that is out there. In the meantime, it helps to live by Ilse's creed: one can find goodness everywhere, even in the heart of evil.

≈≈5/12/01≈≈

Meeting the Other, Finding It's Me

The guys drop us off at the edge of the park while they go to park the car, a not uncommon practice while the four of us cruise the highlights of a few Mexican cities, just for fun. Currently it is Guadalajara we are skimming and we are heading, once the elusive parking spot is found, towards the giant Orozco murals on the walls and ceilings of the Cultural Institute Cardeñas. Finding enough exercise inside the museums, we two happily alight from the car and force our way across the teeming roadway, stepping foot in the park before we realize we are not entering one of the city's tourist attractions.

A searching glance reveals our error: no laughing women and children here, no sleeping tied across their young mothers' breasts, no intertwined couples, no vendors of colorful balloons or marching windup toys, no shoeshine men, no kiosks selling skewered fruit and sugared sweets. No, this is a poor and altogether drab park filled with male derelicts, homeless jobless men (not one woman is in view) in various permutations, some stretched out sleeping on benches, their belongings wrapped in ragged blankets across their , while others huddle in small clusters to share cigarettes and the daily news. The few trees too are spindly and uncared for, dead wood crying to be trimmed. Only a few crimson blossoms scattered here and there on the branches leave room for hope. The few benches are primitive, made of rough, coarse unfinished wooden slats of uneven formation that provide irregular and uninviting seating surfaces.

My elegant friend will have none of this. She would jump back into the car if she could but the car is gone. Seeing there is no escape, she walks regally towards an isolated untenanted bench warmed somewhat by the midmorning sun and sits down tentatively at the edge; I stand before her as if to protect her from an onslaught of ordinary folk. We look around and meet the eyes of a small dark shabbily clothed Mexican walking hurriedly towards us with a gigantic smile on his face.

"Don't talk to him," says my friend, standing up. "Don't say a word." But I have looked into his eyes. How can I ignore him?

"*Buenas dias,*" I reply to his similar greeting, and am ensnared. He has his hand stretched out towards me and asks for money. I have none and say so, in my limited Spanish. But I don't turn away. He is quite lovable and soon another lankier fellow comes along to join in the appeal. They both reek of tequila, maybe a little wine and tobacco as well, as they ask for money in the friendliest of fashions. Not a bit discouraged by getting nothing but a smile in return, they ask where am from. Houston? Dallas? They know the names of the cities where the people with money live.

"No," I say. "St. Louis." They are ecstatic with that bit of information.

"Ah. St. Lou-ees, St. Lou-ees, Colo-rado!" they shout in unison, showing off their knowledge of geography north of the border.

"No. No," I say. "Mizz-oo-ri, St. Lou-ees, Mizz-oo-ri," giving my home state the benefit of a Spanish accent to make it more comprehensible to them, and they love it, repeating the word, in even greater ecstasy of discovery and learning.

They no longer want money. They want talking and that I can give them. I can't give you anything but love, baby, I think, and smile, at myself as much as them. I am only too aware what a picture we make, we three disparate souls having this amicable conversation, with gestures and exclamations, in full view of the world. My girlfriend (if you can call a woman in her seventies that, but that's where we are in time, my girl friend and I) has not only wandered away but has her back to me. She can't watch. As if I were doing some-thing dangerous, risky to life and limb. I ignore her.

"You are beautiful," he says to me, the little one with the big eyes and the ragged clothes and before I realize what he is about to do, he takes my hand and kisses it, cavalierly, humbly, nobly, like a courtier newly stepping on my land and begging for my sanction. I am not a bit offended. On the contrary, I am touched and more than a little embarrassed that he must be humiliated by the degradations of poverty and I, through pure luck and good fortune, am not.

"I love you," he says in English, those dark serious eyes boring into mine with such intensity that I have to believe him and of course I do. It happens that I require a lot of love and it pleases me to believe that he loves me, if only for the moment, with all his heart. When I say, not to be outdone in lovingness or in linguistic aptitude, "*Yo te amo*," his entire body is convulsed with happiness. We are clearly two of a kind.

There are more questions, polite inquiries. His amigo wants us to hire him, I gather, to "help" with something, anything, with which we need help, all kinds of possibilities described in a charming Spanish I don't fully understand. I say no to everything but stay in place, still smiling, still talking, despite the stares from their friends and mine.

I don't know what to do with them, to honor their presence. I have nothing to give beyond my attention to these two mendicants, standing before me like poor men stand, partly bent by their burdens. Their backs are curved by infirmity, disability, lack of food and lack of medical care and, most likely, lack of respect. My admirer leans a bit to the left, the lifelong consequence of a broken leg not set, an ankle stiffened by untreated infection, or some other serious neglect occasioned by deprivation, surely not from lack of love; he is too sweet and affectionate not to have had a loving mother caring for him in the best way she could.

As we talk, a man walks onto the scene carrying a bulging black plastic garbage bag and suddenly, before he comes to a stop, hundreds of birds fly in from all directions in a storm of color that converges before him, almost obscuring the crusts of bread he takes out and tosses to the ground. A mass of rapidly fluttering wings comes to a dynamic rest on the ground before his feet which is quickly converted into a living shimmering carpet of multicolored feathers bobbing for bread. Just as quickly, the bag is emptied and the smiling man folds it up and tucks it in his pocket, his morning ritual complete.

Just as I am wishing I had my hands on a similar magical bag from which to fill the hungry creatures that have flocked to me, my friends call out that it is time to move on.

"Did you have a good time?" they ask with heavy sarcasm when I obey their summons. They don't get me at all.

They can laugh all they want. I did have a good time. There's nothing they can show me I will enjoy more than I have enjoyed my interaction with these loving new friends.

≈≈6/9/03≈≈

The Appeal of Unconsciousness

The sun is shining, flowers are blooming before my eyes and life is wonderful. Every day I find myself becoming more like my mother who has long displayed an amazing ability to put out of mind, instantaneously and forever, any-thing bad that has ever happened. Like her, I now have a subconscious barrier that filters out from my perception all the bad things, the scary things, that happen around us.

So I am happy too, just the way she is. I am on top of the world, my life is nothing but peaches and cream, as I told an intimate recently when she was bemoaning the sadnesses surrounding her. I meant it too. At the moment I said it I honestly felt that everything is good in my life, that I could not think of a thing in the world to worry about. The statement astonished me as it slipped out, sounding almost arrogant in my shallow self-positioning among the wise ones who know no grief, who are able to transcend the small and large disappointments of human existence, which I had for the moment completely and totally forgotten.

Then a friend took me to a pre-release showing of *The Pianist*, the Roman Polanski excursion into the suffering of one human being during the Holocaust. In no time it took me to the place I don't want to go, the place where life has no meaning, where pain and suffering are ubiquitous, all-consuming, where happiness is an ethereal construct without value, where it takes more strength than I have just to keep on watching the cinematic expression of one person's truth.

No sooner is the cinematic curtain opened than I am able to torment myself with my own truths, the ones I don't want to face and in the course of my idyllic daily life, don't have to face. Had I not been safely whisked away from the scene of the horrors against the Jews early on, before men, women and children were corralled for extermination, I would not have had the courage to escape, to live alone in the wreckage of a city, to scrounge and hide and live in constant fear of discovery like this film's protagonist. Instead, I would have died. I know it. Instantly, at the first crisis, I would have died of shock, of fear, of total systemic collapse. Nor would I have had the courage to live, to keep on living, if I had had the opportunity to keep on living, in the ghastly camps, in the crowded trains carrying human beings to the camps, or in any of the then available venues for watching and witnessing the bestiality, the humiliation, the cruelty of the oppressors. I would not have had the courage to live, leaving out of the question entirely the possibility of doing, or killing, or taking action, the way a lot of people who weren't there think Jews should have responded to their maltreatment.

I can barely muster the courage to watch the movie and its fictionalized account of one man's struggle for survival. It is a fiction, I say to myself. You can watch this. Yes, I answer myself. But what if it were not? What would you do? Would you watch then, or would you act? How shamefully would you behave? I don't know the answer to that question. I don't even know the proper standard of behavior from which I know I would surely deviate. Is courage required? If brutes with all the power are wielding force against your babies, your elderly parents, your own irreplaceable fragile body, are you honor-bound to be courageous, or is it acceptable to simply explode, shattering your delicate parts by sheer force of will and whirling, mounting terror?

As I sit and watch the movie, my clammy hand covering my mouth to keep my sighs from growing into moans, I am certain that I would have shattered, splintered myself into the firmament, or wanted to. It was a struggle not to explode right there, in the plush seat of my suburban cinema.

But I didn't. I held myself together and watched the film to the end. And carefully tucked the experience away, slipping back into comfortable unconsciousness. It is the best defense I know. By the time I filed out of the movie theater, surrounded by amateur film critics judging the film on its cinematic merit, I bore no visible trace of internal crisis. With little effort, I was able, on a conscious level, to chat superficially with my friend, and to rejoice, one level of awareness down, that I was able to present a normal facade to the world.

I was still reveling in my unconsciousness when, the very next day, I tripped across these words by Aviva Zornberg[*] in a commentary on the hard-heartedness of the Egyptian Pharaoh that Moses sought to win over to his perspective. Moses is browbeating Pharaoh with predictions of doom if he does not let Moses and his people go:

Pharaoh unhearing, unspeaking, orifices sealed, represents a powerful longing, the "desire to remain unconscious," as Neumann terms it, only to correct himself: "even this is a false formulation, since it starts from consciousness as though that were the natural and self-evident thing. But fixation in unconsciousness, the downward drag of its specific gravity, cannot be called a desire to remain unconscious; on the contrary, that is the natural thing. . . one is primarily unconscious and can at most conquer the original situation in which man drowses in the world, drowses in the unconscious, contained in the infinite like a fish

---

[*] Avivah Gottlieb Zornberg, The *Particulars of Rapture*, p. *103* citing Erich Neumann, *The Origins and History of Consciousness*, New Jersey, Princeton University Press, 1973

in the environing sea.

And so I find that, if Neumann is right, it is not only I, belatedly emulating my mother in a practice I had long considered irrational, but mankind as a whole that is prey to widespread unconsciousness. Giving in to it is natural, and consciousness is what is unnatural. No wonder: consciousness is painful, requiring us to confront the ugliness within and without ourselves.

I like the use of his simile, using the fish in the sea to represent our normal state within the infinite. That we are inclined to swim about, searching for the tidbits available to satisfy our needs, our hungers, without seeing too far beyond the various spaces we occupy seems a fairly realistic observation. But while swimming thoughtlessly in the infinite may be instinctive for most people, it is far different than my way, which has, until now, been closer to the path of excessive consciousness. Dropped into the infinite environing sea, I am the fish caught in the net of constant self-doubt, self-questioning: Is my way the right one? is my heart too hard? is it my fault that something, everything, has gone wrong? do I/we Jews deserve the hatred of the world? am I/are we as good as I/we ought to be? is this all there is?

I would have given up this superconscious, hyperintrospective approach long ago if I'd known how. As an adolescent, reflecting on the evils I had seen committed by the Fatherland, I was already recasting Descartes to bemoan the fact that I think, therefore I am not. A little less consciousness and I would have been a lot more contented. For a person who can't stop thinking, life can be good only as long as one is unconscious of the unmet needs of others. So here I am, way past maturity and happier than I've ever been, with everything in the world I need in the way of material possessions, a free and easy life-style untroubled by past or current problems, personal or familial, plus a loving family and a caring community to support me in my world view, and life **is** good within my own little cocoon. It is only outside it that I see the cruelty of war blazing in the middle east, the poverty and desperation of people in our cities and in distant lands, and the threat of terror and destruction at the hands of zealots all over the world who hate us.

So here I am, way past maturity and happier than I've ever been, with everything in the world I need in the way of material possessions, a free and easy lifestyle untroubled by past or current problems, personal or familial, plus a loving family and a caring community to support me in my world view, and life **is** good within my own little cocoon. It is only outside it that I see the cruelty of war blazing in the middle east, the poverty and desperation of people in our cities and in distant lands, and the threat of terror and destruction at the hands of zealots all over the world who hate us.

Since I can't make it all go away, it comes down to a choice between polar opposites: consciousness or contentment. For the moment, I'm trying contentment on for size.

I like it, it feels good, but I am not altogether sure it fits me.

≈≈1/18/05≈≈

essays

Eschstrasse 19

I was almost over it, the ceaseless obsession I had with the ravages of the Holocaust. In the sixty-some-odd years since my nuclear family escaped unharmed from the nation that felt itself contaminated by our Jewish blood, I had written about it so much that everyone, myself included, thought it unlikely I could ever write on another theme. I had expressed every facet of my personal experience, bland and innocent as it was, and expressed every nuance of my bitter reflections on the human capacity for inflicting pain and cruelty on one another. I had nothing left to say and I was glad. I was done, exhausted by the theme, didn't want to touch it again, ever. I dreamed of writing pieces that would offer light rather than pain.

Once I dropped the burden I had been shlepping around with me for most of my life, I felt lighter. For the first time, I began to flirt with happiness, as if I had a right to it, like ordinary people. I was seeing glasses full, skies bright. And then the letter came, straight from the past, from the dark side. In a wrinkled envelope that betrayed no hint of its contents, came a letter that opened up Pandora's box again. It was forwarded to me by a cousin I hear from sporadically. He had been to Germany several times to visit our mutual hometown and now he mailed me a copy of a letter that he thought might interest me.

essays

That was all he added, that little phrase, "this might interest you," in his scrawled annotation to a letter by a German woman whose name meant nothing and whose return address in Friedrichshafen, Germany, was equally bereft of meaning. It was written to another woman with an Anglican name I also did not know. And it was written in German.

I stared at the paper, begging it for easy answers. I had no idea who these people were and the prospect of working my way through the inscrutable German words was intimidating. It would be a daunting task: I had rejected the use of that enemy language as a child when I wanted nothing more than to be all-American, all the time. But just looking at the jumble of German words revealed my own name here and there and, inevitably, curiosity overcame trepidation. I pulled out my large German-English dictionary, set to work, and soon discovered that the bulk of the letter comprised the writer's account of Kristallnacht, detailing her memory of what had happened to her Jewish neighbors on the night when the first organized battle against the Jews of Germany took place. It is an occurrence close to my heart about which I have thought many times.

Persevering past the linguistic obstacles, I found, to my complete amazement, that the story being told was my story, the story of my family on that dismal November night in 1938. She was writing in November 2003 in response to a request by a dedicated Scottish woman who had taken on the project of leading high school students in Bünde, Westfphalia, to research their communal history in order to uncover the truth about the fate of the resident Jews in their hometown and mine.

Until Christina Whitelaw undertook her mission, the general understanding was that nothing bad had ever happened there. The Jews had just left. No one had bothered them. She suspected otherwise. But this I learned later; when the letter came, I had no idea to

essays

whom Bärbel was writing. "My dear Mrs. Whitelaw," she wrote on an old-fashioned typewriter, the typing errors visible, uncorrected by modern technology. In German, she wrote:

> The first personal experience that filled me with fear and horror was that of Kristallnacht. It was about seven pm, my father was not yet home. My mother was busy in the kitchen where I was playing. House and apartment doors were in those days always open. Suddenly we heard a commotion of thudding and clanking with the trampling of boots coming near, and saw SS people in their black uniforms advancing over the floor and living space into our kitchen, shouting: 'Does Spiegel live here?'

That is my father she is talking about. My father. I can barely go on reading. As if I did not know the story. But Bärbel reports:
My mother said, 'No, not here' and, noting her Aryan appearance (she was blond and I was light blond), the officers turned about and left.

I felt faint as I read these few sentences. This woman not only remembered my family after more than six decades but was telling my story of Kristallnacht with some of the same details I employ in telling it. Who could she be? Why did I not know her name? I still knew the name of the Storm Trooper's daughter who lived on the top floor (unforgettable because of her habit of standing always with her skirt hiked up on her right side while she held on to the bottom edge of her underpants) but Bärbel Eyrich, the name signed on the letter, that name stirred no memory whatsoever.

It was Saturday afternoon when the letter arrived and left me dumbfounded. It was early evening, I was preparing to go out for dinner with my husband and friends, standing in front of my vanity mirror, looking at

essays

my aging reflection, wondering who this letter writer could be, when I had a flash of recollection.

"I think I have something...," I mumbled and rushed to dig out of my file cabinet a slim folder that held a very few papers from my childhood, among them a thin little navy blue notebook which I now pulled out. It had crossed the ocean with me. I hadn't looked at in years. On its outside a white label bears my name written in my small, careful German script: MIRJAM SPIEGEL.

On the inside only one of the double-lined pages has writing on it, mine, in my new English cursive. I was eight, starting over in first grade in order to learn to write, and speak, the new language. I wrote this tiny story in April 1939, just a month after our arrival in America; now it is the only record of my thoughts as a newly displaced young person, suddenly lost in the land of milk and honey.

Reflecting on what I had left behind, I wrote, under the heading of "The good girl in germany [sic],"

> I had a friend whose mother and father are good people. My friend's name is Bärbel, she is five years old. She lives in "Bünde/Westfalia". I am very fond of Bärbel. She has a big doll and a bed for the doll. That is nice.

It was difficult to believe the evidence in my hands, persuasive evidence that this woman living in Germany who didn't know I was alive and was telling my story as her own, was Bärbel, my childhood friend, of whom I had not had a thought in sixty-four years. Whom I had actually forgotten, totally, despite the fact that I had thought enough of her to describe her as a "good girl," surely a heavily laden term for one newly escaped from Nazi oppression. That is enough to take my breath away. When Bärbel's report gets around to me, she says:

essays

The daughter, Mirjam, was a few years older than I, she was already in school, but she was my playmate, *i.e.*, I was allowed to play with her still, while the other children of the residents would sing around the sandbox: 'Two Jews were sitting on a bench!......' Mirjam was a clean and well behaved child...

I was seven when she was five, and she remembers our play times and the still familiar details of antisemitic taunts (she knows the whole ditty but stops herself from providing all its words), and that I was well-behaved, but "clean"? Why in the world would she describe me as clean? Why would that descriptive even come to mind? unless it was in denial of the extant Germanic stereotype lingering in her mind? Well, one has to deal with the world as it is.

She remembers our playing in the sandbox together. I have photographs of me in that very sandbox, and a jagged scar on my thigh where once an old metal sand bucket drew blood while I was playing there and I cried in pain. That suddenly comes to life again. I am that little girl again, playing fantasy beach games in a square wooden box on the grass of the back garden of the house with my friend.

And now I feel for the first time what "good people" they really were, that mother and father of Bärbel's who permitted her to play with me even while others reviled or teased me. But I did know it, even at eight, and thought it important enough to mention it prominently in my "story," as if I knew, as she wrote in another part of her letter, that her parents had always opposed the Nazis. How grateful I am. Now, when it is too late to thank them for their courage.

There was more information in the letter, facts I hadn't known, including the name and unfortunate fate of the German citizen who had bought my dad's business under the pressure of laws prohibiting Jewish business ownership. When the destroyers came on Kristallnacht, his claim of ownership had prevented its destruction even while our home was ransacked. The business was located in the rear house, which, she wrote, "stands still today; the front house, in which we lived, was razed and rebuilt new, Eschstrasse 19." It was where our home and business stood under one roof.

And then she wrote, and of this I had no clue, that after our apartment was totally destroyed, her parents had examined the ravages, and "the male residents then searched the house from roof to cellar, in the fear that Herr Spiegel had taken his life."

Who knew that they too were worried when we were scared to death we would never see him again? Who suspected that they shared at least a fraction of our anxiety?

What strange things happen in the world. One can never cease to be amazed by the wonderful, ordinary events that happen. How likely was it that we two, truly long-lost friends, would find one another again? and by accident? without trying? Surely the statistical probability of such an event occurring is infinitesimal. I am grateful that it did.

Only now that we have exchanged a few letters, have overcome the initial hesitations, and have resumed a tentative relationship, it is clear to me how much she, as a Christian child in a pagan land, must have suffered during those long years of war and deprivation, hunger and cold. There, across the sea, in the brutal land I did everything in my power to forget, she was having her own lonely struggle to find meaning and happiness. I should never have forgotten her.

After all, after all is said and done and said again, it is the good people, not Amalek, that we must remember, and then, aim to match their virtue.

≈≈6/05/2006≈≈

essays

Coda

". . . And when the event, the big change in your life, is simply an insight -- isn't that a strange thing? That absolutely nothing changes except that you see things differently and you're less fearful and less anxious and generally stronger as a result: isn't it amazing that a completely invisible thing in your head can feel realer than anything that you've experienced before? You see things more clearly and you know that you're seeing them more clearly. And it comes to you that this is what it means to love life, this is all anybody who talks seriously about God is ever talking about. Moments like this. . . . "

Jonathan Franzen, in *The Corrections*

1459872

Made in the USA